Practical GPU Programming

High-performance computing with CUDA, CuPy, and Python on modern GPUs

Maris Fenlor

Published by: GitforGits

Publisher: Sonal Dhandre

www.gitforgits.com

Printed in India

First Printing: February 2025

ISBN: 978-93-49174-79-5

Cover Design by: Kitten Publishing

Prologue

I recall a time when running applications that used a lot of data meant getting the most out of the CPU. For years, we thought that faster processors and more cores would solve our problems in scientific computing, analytics, and simulation. But as our data sets got bigger and our algorithms got more complex, even the most powerful CPUs couldn't keep up. Eventually, I came to see that the future of computing wasn't going to be defined by just the CPU. GPUs, which were originally designed for rendering graphics in video games, have become the true engines of modern computational progress. They're so powerful that they can run thousands of operations at once and totally changed the game for high-performance computing. It was cool to see researchers speeding up genomics and drug discovery, data engineers cranking out machine learning pipelines, and engineers simulating physical stuff with equipment they could fit under their desks.

While the potential of GPU computing was certainly promising, I also saw that it was still quite challenging to take advantage of it. Most of us were raised on serial programming with a focus on the CPU. When I first looked at CUDA, memory hierarchies, or kernel launches, I found myself struggling to connect these powerful new tools with my day-to-day workflows in Python. The learning curve felt steep, and it was easy to get lost in the details of memory management, thread scheduling, or obscure hardware limitations. I wrote it because I think the future is going to be all about people who can switch easily between high-level application logic and the raw speed of GPU acceleration. I want to show you that you don't have to choose between performance and productivity. If you're careful about how you do it, you can keep writing code in Python and use tools like CUDA, PyCUDA, and CuPy.

In this book, I'll be talking about parallel processing, high-performance computing, memory management, and kernel optimization. I'll be focusing on real code, live demonstrations, and hands-on projects. In this book, we'll work on practical tasks like sorting, searching, and linear algebra. You'll see how the GPU works and why these skills matter for your everyday problems. You'll learn how to combine PyCUDA's precision with CuPy's ease of use, and how to take the best of both worlds and apply them in a single workflow. I want you to see each new concept as a tool you can use, not just another piece of theory. Whenever we run into something tricky, like a memory bottleneck, a tricky kernel bug, or a performance tradeoff, I'll show you how to break it down, test it, and solve it with code you can actually run.

By the time you're done with this book, you'll have the confidence and the skills to do GPU programming tasks that were once only for experts. The future of computing isn't just about faster chips; it's about finding smarter ways to do computation. No matter what your title is, I want you to join me in building that future, one line of GPU-powered Python at a time.

— Maris Fenlor

Content

Preface

If you're a Python pro looking to get the most out of your code with GPUs, then Practical GPU Programming is the right book for you. This book will walk you through the basics of GPU architectures, show you hands-on parallel programming techniques, and give you the know-how to confidently speed up real workloads in data processing, analytics, and engineering.

The first thing you'll do is set up the environment, install CUDA, and get a handle on using Python libraries like PyCUDA and CuPy. You'll then dive into memory management, kernel execution, and parallel patterns like reductions and histogram computations. Then, we'll dive into sorting and search techniques, but with a focus on how GPU acceleration transforms business data processing. We'll also put a strong emphasis on linear algebra to show you how to supercharge classic vector and matrix operations with cuBLAS and CuPy. Plus, with batched computations, efficient broadcasting, custom kernels, and mixed-library workflows, you can tackle both standard and advanced problems with ease.

Throughout, we evaluate numerical accuracy and performance side by side, so you can understand both the strengths and limitations of GPU-based solutions. The book covers nearly every essential skill and modern toolkit for practical GPU programming, but it's not going to turn you into a master overnight.

In this book we will learn how to:

- Boost processing speed and efficiency for data-intensive tasks.
- Use CuPy and PyCUDA to write and execute custom CUDA kernels.
- Maximize GPU occupancy and throughput efficiency by using optimal thread block and grid configuration.
- Reduce global memory bottlenecks in kernels by using shared memory and coalesced access patterns.
- Perform dynamic kernel compilation to ensure tailored performance.
- Use CuPy to carry out custom, high-speed elementwise GPU operations and expressions.
- Implement bitonic and radix sort algorithms for large or batch integer datasets.
- Execute parallel linear search kernels to detect patterns rapidly.
- Scale matrix operations using Batched GEMM and high-level cuBLAS routines.

GitforGits

Prerequisites

Even if you're a total newbie to the world of GPUs, this book will take you from the basics of CPUs to the current world of GPU programming. All you need is some Python experience and a willingness to explore and try the techniques it offers.

Codes Usage

Are we in need of some helpful code examples to assist we in our programming and documentation? Look no further! Our book offers a wealth of supplemental material, including code examples and exercises.

Not only is this book here to aid we in getting our job done, but we have our permission to use the example code in our programs and documentation. However, please note that if we are reproducing a significant portion of the code, we do require we to contact us for permission.

But don't worry, using several chunks of code from this book in our program or answering a question by citing our book and quoting example code does not require permission. But if we do choose to give credit, an attribution typically includes the title, author, publisher, and ISBN. For example, "Practical GPU Programming by Maris Fenlor".

If we are unsure whether our intended use of the code examples falls under fair use or the permissions outlined above, please do not hesitate to reach out to us at support@gitforgits.com.

We are happy to assist and clarify any concerns.

Acknowledgement

I owe a tremendous debt of gratitude to GitforGits, for their unflagging enthusiasm and wise counsel throughout the entire process of writing this book. Their knowledge and careful editing helped make sure the piece was useful for people of all reading levels and comprehension skills. In addition, I'd like to thank everyone involved in the publishing process for their efforts in making this book a reality. Their efforts, from copyediting to advertising, made the project what it is today.

Finally, I'd like to express my gratitude to everyone who has shown me unconditional love and encouragement throughout my life. Their support was crucial to the completion of this book. I appreciate our help with this endeavour and our continued interest in my career.

CHAPTER 1: INTRODUCTION TO GPU FUNDAMENTALS

GPU versus CPU for Data Processing

An era is found in which every field—science, business, engineering, media, and even our day-to-day web browsing—is reliant on ever-growing volumes of data. The days when a single desktop or server CPU could handle an entire workflow are fading. So, as we start moving from megabytes to gigabytes and then to terabytes of data, we will see that our scripts and applications are really struggling to keep up. This isn't just about size; it's about how complicated it is, how fast it is, and how important it is to get results right away.

Our tasks may involve processing medical images, transforming large data sets for analytics, training or deploying neural networks, running simulations, or streaming video to millions of people. CPUs, even with multiple cores, weren't designed for these massive amounts of parallel, repetitive work. You may have started to hear more about GPU acceleration and how it can unlock almost magical performance, shrinking jobs that took hours to mere minutes or even seconds.

Before we start writing code, we should know why the world is moving from CPU to GPU for so many apps. This first topic will help we understand the main forces, the differences in hardware, and the practical impact on our daily data challenges.

How CPUs and GPUs Process Data?

The central processing unit of a computer system is frequently referred to as the "brain" of the apparatus. It is extremely versatile, capable of complex decision-making, running entire operating systems, and managing dozens of software threads simultaneously. A CPU core is powerful and flexible. It is equipped with sophisticated control logic, huge caches, and a very high clock speed. Most CPUs in desktops and servers today have between four and 64 cores, each of which can process independent streams of instructions.

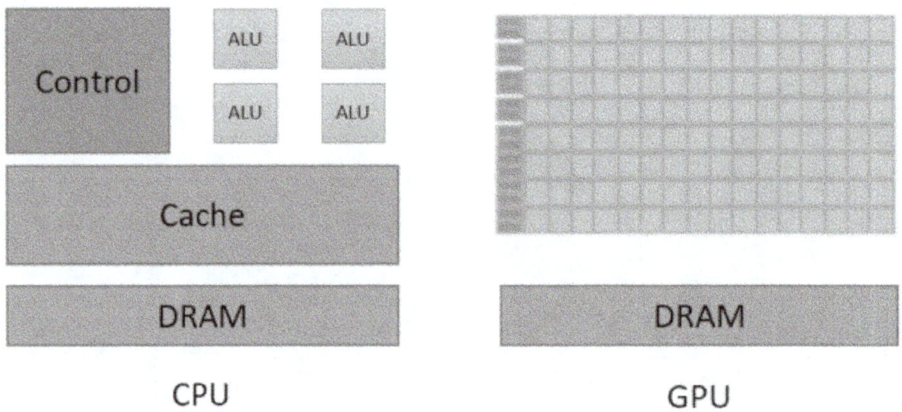

Fig 1.1 CPU vs. GPU

(Source: https://developer.nvidia.com/blog/cuda-refresher-reviewing-the-origins-of-gpu-computing)

However, CPUs are optimized for sequential processing. You may find that our code spends much of its time in loops or single-threaded routines, areas in which the CPU excels. But when working with massive arrays—such as filtering a billion image pixels or multiplying huge matrices—the CPU's design reveals its limitations. Though fast, each core can only process so many instructions per second. Adding more cores helps, but we quickly reach a point of diminishing returns.

On the other hand, a radically different approach is taken by a GPU—Graphics Processing Unit. So, instead of having a few "smart" cores, it's got thousands of simple, lightweight cores that are designed to work together. While each GPU core isn't as powerful as a CPU core individually, they excel at performing the same operation across huge blocks of data simultaneously. This is called single instruction, multiple data (SIMD) parallelism.

Limits of CPU Scaling

One might wonder: Why can't we just add more CPU cores? After all, server CPUs now ship with dozens of cores, and cloud providers offer machines with hundreds of virtual CPUs (vCPUs). However, the issue is more complex than simply "more is better."

First, CPUs are expensive to scale. Each core requires complex control units and large, low-latency caches, which take up significant silicon space and require a lot of power. Second, as we add more cores, we run into Amdahl's law—the idea that our program is only as fast as its slowest, most sequential part. Unless every part of our code can run independently, there will always be bottlenecks that prevent the system from scaling perfectly.

For example, we might have written multithreaded Python scripts using libraries like threading or multiprocessing. As we increase the number of threads, we will quickly notice that global locks, thread contention, and the infamous Global Interpreter Lock (GIL) limit the benefits. The process of transferring data between threads results in overhead, thereby reducing the available memory bandwidth. In practice, CPUs can handle tens of parallel threads, but not thousands.

GPUs Outshine CPUs

This is precisely where the GPU comes into play. Imagine working with a 4,000-by-4,000-pixel image. If we want to apply a transformation to every pixel, we have 16 million independent computations. This could include adjusting brightness or applying a filter. Even with 16 or 32 cores, a CPU would have to divide this workload and spread it across a small number of threads. The overhead of managing so many small tasks and shuffling data between cores would be significant.

However, a GPU is built for this exact task. With thousands of computing cores, the GPU assigns each pixel's operation to its own thread. Suddenly, the entire image can be processed in parallel, as if each pixel had its own processor. The difference is clear in the numbers: workloads that would take the CPU many seconds can be completed in a fraction of a second on a GPU. This architecture isn't just good for graphics. The GPU's parallel capabilities can be a boon for any workload that follows the "same operation, many data points" paradigm. This includes scientific computing, neural network inference, statistical simulations, and large-scale data analytics.

Closer Look at the Hardware

To make the most of GPU programming, it helps to know a little about what's inside the hardware. A modern CPU might have 8–32 cores, each running at 3–4 GHz, with a complex pipeline and several megabytes of cache. In contrast, a typical NVIDIA GPU could feature 5,000 to 10,000 simple CUDA cores, running at lower clock speeds but grouped into Streaming Multiprocessors (SMs). Each SM schedules and manages groups of 32 threads, called warps, and the hardware can keep many warps "in flight" at once.

GPUs connect to the rest of the system via PCI Express, which, while fast, is still much slower than the on-chip memory bandwidth. You have access to several memory types on the GPU: global memory (large, high-latency, high-bandwidth), shared memory (small, low-latency, within an SM), and registers (ultra-fast, per-thread). The hardware is designed to maximize throughput; meaning the total amount of data processed per second, by hiding memory latency and overlapping computation with data movement.

Why GPU Programming Matters Now?

If we have worked mostly in Python, we know how easy it is to manipulate data with libraries like NumPy or pandas. As our data grows, we find that NumPy operations become slow, especially for operations like large matrix multiplication, reductions, or elementwise computations over huge arrays. GPU programming used to be reserved for those willing to dive into C++ and complex CUDA APIs. Thankfully, libraries like CuPy and PyCUDA now bring GPU power directly to our Python code, making parallel computing accessible with familiar syntax. You can often take code written for NumPy, swap out the import statement, and see dramatic speedups—all while staying in our Python comfort zone.

Machine Learning and Deep Learning Inference

Suppose we are deploying a neural network that processes thousands of images per second for object detection or classification. The forward pass of a deep neural network consists of many large matrix multiplications and elementwise activations. CPUs cannot deliver real-time inference at this scale without massive clusters. GPUs, designed for parallel floating-point operations, deliver results in a fraction of the time, supporting large-scale AI services from the cloud to the edge.

High-Performance Data Analytics

You may work on ETL pipelines, process logs, or run statistical analysis on millions of records. Tasks like grouping, aggregation, filtering, and histogram computation map perfectly to the GPU's strengths. Python libraries such as RAPIDS and CuDF leverage the GPU for database-style operations, letting we accelerate analytics workloads far beyond what a CPU can offer.

Real-Time Visualization and Rendering

Interactive visualizations, 3D rendering, and gaming all rely on the GPU's ability to update millions of pixels dozens of times per second. But even outside graphics, scientists and engineers use GPUs to visualize simulation results, plot large point clouds, or animate molecular dynamics. CPUs simply can't keep up with these demanding, highly parallel workloads.

Scientific Computing and Simulations

Physical simulations—weather models, fluid dynamics, Monte Carlo simulations—require updating the state of millions of particles or grid points. GPUs excel at these embarrassingly parallel problems, letting we run more accurate or higher-resolution models without waiting hours for results.

When we run code on a GPU, we don't always get a 1000× speedup. The key is matching our workload to the hardware's strengths. For large enough arrays, we can expect 10× to 100× acceleration for common tasks like vector addition, matrix multiplication, and reductions. For smaller data, the overhead of moving data to and from the GPU may erase any benefit.

To see this for yourself, we will soon run a benchmark in Python, comparing a simple array operation on the CPU (NumPy) and GPU (CuPy). By plotting runtime versus array size, we discover that the GPU "wins" decisively for large data, while the CPU is sometimes faster for small tasks where transfer overhead dominates.

What Makes GPU Programming Different?

The GPU excels at workloads with these characteristics:

- Operations are the same across many data points (data parallelism)
- Each computation is independent (little to no inter-thread communication)
- You need to process large datasets, not just a few items

Where GPUs don't excel: workloads that are inherently sequential, heavily reliant on complex branching, or require constant communication between threads. For those, our CPU remains essential.

As we move into GPU programming, we shift our mindset. You stop thinking about "one operation at a time" and instead ask, "Can I write this in a way that all elements run together?" You start to care about memory layout, coalescing, and how to structure work to minimize waiting. In Python, we get much of this automatically with CuPy or PyCUDA, but we will see even better results when we understand how to align our algorithms to the hardware.

Ther are common questions and some of the real concerns that keeps coming to our mind such as,

- will GPU programming always help?
- Isn't it hard to learn GPU programming?

- Will my code run everywhere?
- Can I use GPU and CPU together?

The answer to all such questions are very simple. At first we must consider data size and algorithm structure. If our arrays are small or our algorithm is highly sequential, CPU may be best. But as soon as our data grows or our computations can be described as "do the same thing for every row," GPU shines. If we stick to modern Python libraries, we won't need to write low-level CUDA C code unless we want to. We will get familiar, high-level APIs that feel like NumPy. This book will show you, step-by-step, how to move from basic data structures to launching our own GPU kernels.

We will also need a compatible GPU (usually NVIDIA for CUDA-based libraries) and the right drivers. For many cloud providers, GPU instances are a click away. Even consumer laptops often have CUDA-capable hardware. Once our environment is set up, the workflow is as seamless as any Python project. And we must remember that many workloads use the CPU for orchestration, complex logic, and data preparation, while the GPU handles heavy lifting. We will often copy data to the GPU, run the kernel, and copy results back. Such hybrid workflows are common in scientific computing and machine learning.

Let's Get Started!

We are about to take our first steps into actual coding by benchmarking the CPU versus the GPU for a simple operation. You will see the entire workflow: creating data in Python, processing it on the CPU, and running the same logic on the GPU using CuPy or PyCUDA. You will compare runtimes, verify correctness, and learn to interpret our results. The tone for the entire book is set by this hands-on approach. Each concept is connected to a specific coding task that we can run and modify on our own machine. As we move forward, we will learn to understand which operations to outsource and how to improve memory movement and kernel configuration.

You're at the beginning of a practical path that will change how we approach high-performance computing in Python. We will learn to identify data-parallel opportunities, profile our code, and transition effortlessly between CPU and GPU, empowering we to address modern data challenges with confidence. If you're looking to boost the speed of data pipelines, create machine learning services, or simply want to analyze data more quickly, GPU programming can take we to a whole new level of performance. We will move forward by seeing, in real code, how these ideas translate into real-world speedups.

Streaming Multiprocessor and Core Concepts

You have seen the promise of GPU acceleration, but to harness it fully, we need to understand what's happening inside the hardware. Unlike CPUs, which focus on high clock speeds and sophisticated instruction logic, GPUs organize their resources for parallel throughput. At the heart of every modern GPU lies a set of Streaming Multiprocessors, or SMs. Each SM is a powerhouse built to execute thousands of threads in parallel, using a structure designed to hide latency and keep data moving.

We will break down the anatomy. When we look at a GPU, we find dozens of SMs sitting side by side. Each SM includes a collection of simple CUDA cores (the basic compute units), special function units, registers, shared memory, and the warp scheduler. Think of an SM as a self-contained mini-processor that manages its own pool of threads. The number of SMs varies by GPU model—entry-level cards may have just a few, while data center GPUs boast eighty or more.

How SMs Work?

When we launch a kernel, you're telling the GPU, "This is a huge grid of threads; please execute the same code across all of them." The GPU takes our thread grid and splits it into blocks, each block containing up to a few hundred threads. Each block then gets assigned to an SM. This is where things get interesting: each SM can execute multiple blocks at once, depending on resource availability (registers, shared memory, and so on).

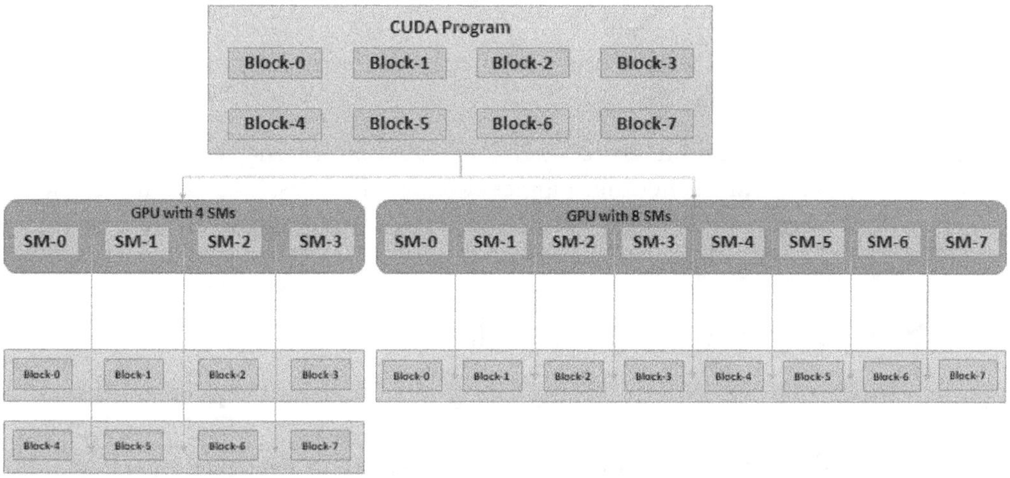

Fig 1.2 CUDA Blocks

(Source: https://developer.nvidia.com/blog/cuda-refresher-getting-started-with-cuda)

Within the SM, threads are further grouped into warps—sets of 32 threads that run in lockstep. Each cycle, the SM's warp scheduler picks one or more active warps and sends them to the CUDA cores for execution. All threads in a warp execute the same instruction at the same time, but operate on different pieces of data. This is the foundation of SIMD (Single Instruction, Multiple Data) programming, which is why GPUs are so efficient at handling large arrays or images.

You might imagine a large classroom where each row (warp) follows the same learning plan, but each student works on their own worksheet. The SM's warp scheduler can manage several of these "rows" at once, quickly switching between them to ensure everyone stays busy, even if some threads need to wait for memory or data.

What is Occupancy?

You will hear the term "occupancy" often in GPU programming. Occupancy measures how effectively we are using the GPU's parallel resources, specifically, how many warps are active on each SM compared to the maximum possible. Higher occupancy means more warps are ready to run, which helps the SM hide memory latency. If one warp gets stalled waiting for data, the scheduler simply switches to another warp.

You can increase occupancy by launching more threads per block, reducing register and shared memory usage per thread, or optimizing our kernel to avoid bottlenecks. However, higher occupancy does not always guarantee better performance—sometimes, we hit a sweet spot that balances resource usage and throughput.

Warp Scheduling and Performance Patterns

The warp scheduler in each SM is like an air traffic controller for parallel execution. It chooses which warps to run based on availability, readiness, and resource constraints. When one warp is waiting on memory or a synchronization point, the scheduler quickly swaps in another warp, keeping the hardware busy. This rapid context switching is lightweight because all the threads and their data remain resident on the SM.

You see the true power of this architecture when handling high-latency operations, such as reading from global memory. The warp scheduler juggles dozens of warps, overlapping computation and data transfer, so the SM never idles. If we structure our code to expose enough parallel work, the scheduler takes care of latency hiding for you.

Running Simple Microbenchmark

We will get hands-on. You can explore SM and warp scheduling concepts using a small PyCUDA or CuPy kernel. Suppose we want to measure how many threads our GPU can handle in parallel, and how execution time changes with different block sizes. This isn't just an academic exercise—it's the first step in tuning our code for high performance.

First, set up an array with millions of elements. Then, write a kernel that performs a trivial operation (like adding a constant) to each element. Launch the kernel with various block sizes (say, 32, 64, 128, 256, 512, and 1024 threads per block) and measure the execution time for each. We will likely observe that some configurations run much faster than others, depending on how well they "fit" our GPU's SM architecture. By printing out the number of SMs and maximum threads per SM using Python queries (CuPy or PyCUDA provide device attributes), we match our launch configuration to the hardware's sweet spot. Try running the same operation with too few threads—your GPU will be underutilized. With too many threads per block, we may run out of registers or shared memory, dropping occupancy and hurting performance.

As we work through these microbenchmarks, several high-performance patterns become clear. First, we want to maximize the number of threads per SM without over-consuming resources.

Second, we prefer to launch enough blocks so every SM stays busy, especially on larger GPUs. Third, we notice the importance of memory coalescing: structuring data access so that threads in a warp read from consecutive memory addresses, boosting throughput. When we put these patterns into practice, even simple kernels for tasks like vector addition or histogram computation see order-of-magnitude speedups over naive implementations.

If we understand SMs, warps, occupancy, and the scheduler, we can feel confident to experiment with launch parameters and kernel resource usage. Instead of just writing code, you're tuning our programs to the rhythm of the hardware. Each kernel we write provides an opportunity to observe the effects of our decisions in real time.

Thread Blocks, Grids and Indexing

I'm sure you've heard of CUDA by now. It's the technology that lets us use the power of NVIDIA GPUs in our own code. CUDA (Compute Unified Device Architecture) provides the framework for launching thousands of lightweight threads on the GPU. With Python, we can use libraries like PyCUDA or CuPy to write code that compiles and runs CUDA kernels, all while staying in the comfort of our usual Python environment. For this book, we're going to use Linux as our default setup since it's got great support for CUDA development.

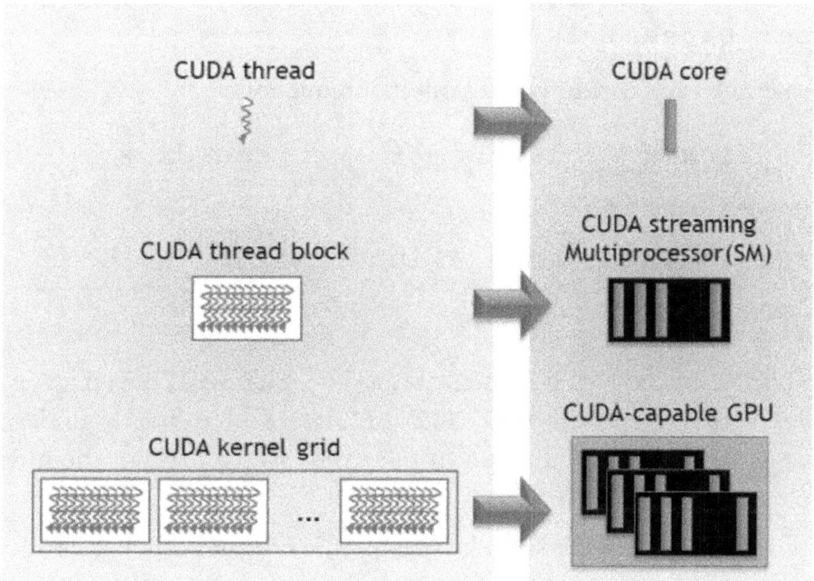

Fig 1.3 GPU-Kernel Execution

(Source: https://developer.nvidia.com/blog/cuda-refresher-cuda-programming-model)

The Thread Hierarchy

In CUDA, parallel work is organized using a two-level hierarchy: **grids** and **blocks**. Each time we launch a kernel, we specify how many blocks to run and how many threads to put in each block. Every thread in the grid executes the same code, but processes a different part of the data. Think of our data like a big spreadsheet. The idea is to assign a team to each region of the spreadsheet, or blocks, and a worker to each cell in that region, or threads. CUDA's architecture lets us process huge datasets: 1D, 2D, or even 3D arrays, by mapping each data element to its own thread in the grid.

Mapping 1D Arrays

To do that, we will need a working Python environment with CUDA support. If this is our first time, then go ahead and install PyCUDA or CuPy in a virtual environment and confirm that our GPU is visible. If we want to check, just import our library and print the device properties. For example, with CuPy:

```
import cupy as cp
print(cp.cuda.runtime.getDeviceProperties(0))
```

After this, we will begin with a simple 1D array. Suppose we have an array with a million elements, and we want each thread to square its assigned element. When we launch our kernel, we decide how many threads per block (say, 256), and how many blocks we will need (**`num_elements // threads_per_block + 1`**).

Inside our CUDA kernel, each thread figures out its unique index:

```
int idx = blockIdx.x * blockDim.x + threadIdx.x;
if (idx < num_elements) {
    output[idx] = input[idx] * input[idx];
}
```

The calculation **`blockIdx.x * blockDim.x + threadIdx.x`** gives every thread a unique global index across the entire grid. The **`if`** statement is our boundary check—some threads might have an index beyond the end of our array, so we prevent them from writing out of bounds.

On the Python side, after running the kernel, we copy the output array back from device to host and check our results:

```
import cupy as cp
num_elements = 1_000_000
input_array = cp.arange(num_elements, dtype=cp.float32)
output_array = cp.empty_like(input_array)
```

```
threads_per_block = 256
blocks_per_grid = (num_elements + threads_per_block - 1) //
threads_per_block
kernel_code = '''
extern "C" __global__
void square(const float *input, float *output, int n) {
    int idx = blockIdx.x * blockDim.x + threadIdx.x;
    if (idx < n) {
        output[idx] = input[idx] * input[idx];
    }
}
'''
module = cp.RawModule(code=kernel_code)
square_kernel = module.get_function('square')
square_kernel((blocks_per_grid,), (threads_per_block,),
              (input_array, output_array, num_elements))
# Copy results to host and verify
result = cp.asnumpy(output_array)
assert (result == (cp.asnumpy(input_array) ** 2)).all()
print("1D kernel executed successfully!")
```

We have just mapped a 1D array onto CUDA's grid and block system.

Mapping 2D Arrays

Now, suppose we want to process a 2D array like an image or a matrix. You need to map rows and columns to two grid dimensions. The CUDA supports multi-dimensional blocks and grids, letting each thread process a single pixel or matrix entry.

Now here, inside our kernel, we need to calculate both the row and column index:

```
int row = blockIdx.y * blockDim.y + threadIdx.y;
int col = blockIdx.x * blockDim.x + threadIdx.x;
if (row < height && col < width) {
```

```
    output[row * width + col] = input[row * width + col] +
1.0f;
}
```

In Python, we can adjust our launch configuration:

```
height, width = 1024, 1024
input_array = cp.random.rand(height, width).astype(cp.float32)
output_array = cp.empty_like(input_array)
block = (16, 16)
grid = ((width + block[0] - 1) // block[0],
        (height + block[1] - 1) // block[1])
kernel_code = '''
extern "C" __global__
void increment(const float *input, float *output, int width,
int height) {
    int col = blockIdx.x * blockDim.x + threadIdx.x;
    int row = blockIdx.y * blockDim.y + threadIdx.y;
    if (row < height && col < width) {
        output[row * width + col] = input[row * width + col] +
1.0f;
    }
}
'''
module = cp.RawModule(code=kernel_code)
increment_kernel = module.get_function('increment')
increment_kernel(grid, block, (input_array, output_array,
width, height))
result = cp.asnumpy(output_array)
assert (result == cp.asnumpy(input_array) + 1).all()
print("2D kernel executed and verified successfully!")
```

After this, each thread computes its row and column. The boundary check ensures we do not run past the edge if the grid size does not perfectly match the array dimensions.

You can extend this pattern to 3D data like, volumetric images or simulation grids. The CUDA lets us specify three-dimensional blocks and grids, and each thread computes a **(z, y, x)** index to process its own voxel or data point. The key is always the same: map the logical data position (whether 1D, 2D, or 3D) to CUDA's thread and block indices, check boundaries, and ensure each thread works only within valid data.

Now that we know this, we can start using custom kernels for any data shape. The basics of mapping Python arrays to CUDA grids and blocks, handling boundaries, and verifying output are already in our toolkit. These patterns will show up in almost every GPU application we build, creating the foundation for real-world high-performance Python code.

Host–Device Interaction Overview

You are about to see firsthand how our Python code communicates with the GPU. This process involves a few core steps: memory allocation, data transfer, launching a kernel, and understanding the different memory spaces involved. You have already installed CuPy, so you're ready to put theory into practice. We will build our intuition by writing a minimal yet complete script that covers all the essentials.

Memory Allocation on GPU

In CuPy, when we allocate an array, you're basically reserving memory directly on the GPU, not on our computer's main RAM. This is a big change in thinking. If we use CuPy, the arrays we create will be saved on the device.

Here's a simple way to do it:

```
import cupy as cp
# Allocate an array of 10,000 floats on the GPU
gpu_array = cp.zeros(10_000, dtype=cp.float32)
print("Array allocated on GPU:", gpu_array)
```

This single line gives we a chunk of GPU memory. Unlike NumPy arrays, these cannot be used directly with CPU-only functions.

Host to Device and Back

The main Python script runs on the CPU (the "host"), but the heavy lifting happens on the GPU (the "device"). To use GPU acceleration, we first need to move our data from the host to the device.

So, first we'll make a NumPy array, and then we'll transfer it to the GPU.

```
import numpy as np
# Create data on the host
host_data = np.arange(10_000, dtype=np.float32)
# Transfer data to the GPU (device)
device_data = cp.asarray(host_data)
print("Data transferred to GPU.")
```

This command moves the entire array to GPU memory. If we want to bring results back, use **cp.asnumpy**:

```
# Bring the data back from device to host
result_on_host = cp.asnumpy(device_data)
print("Data transferred back to host. First five elements:", result_on_host[:5])
```

You will often find yourself moving data back and forth, especially when we need to verify output, save results, or interact with other libraries that require NumPy arrays.

Launching a Simple Kernel

What's really cool about CuPy is that it lets us write custom CUDA kernels right in Python. Let's say there's an array of elements, and we want to multiply each one by two. You can use CuPy's RawKernel interface to write this kernel.

```
kernel_code = r'''
extern "C" __global__
void multiply_by_two(float* data, int n) {
    int idx = blockDim.x * blockIdx.x + threadIdx.x;
    if (idx < n) {
        data[idx] *= 2.0f;
    }
}
'''
```

```
module = cp.RawModule(code=kernel_code)
multiply_by_two = module.get_function('multiply_by_two')
# Set up array and parameters
n = 10_000
threads_per_block = 256
blocks_per_grid = (n + threads_per_block - 1) //
threads_per_block
# Launch the kernel
multiply_by_two((blocks_per_grid,), (threads_per_block,),
(gpu_array, n))
print("Kernel launched to multiply elements by two.")
```

After this, we can transfer our results back to the host and check correctness:

```
# Bring back to host and verify
cpu_result = cp.asnumpy(gpu_array)
print("First five elements after kernel:", cpu_result[:5])
```

Understanding GPU Memory Spaces

So far, you've worked with the two main "memory spaces":

- **Host memory** (your main system RAM) where NumPy arrays live and where our Python script begins.
- And the other is, **Device memory** (the GPU) where CuPy arrays are allocated and where kernels read/write data.

The magic of GPU programming comes from knowing when to move data and where each operation takes place. Most computations on CuPy arrays happen entirely on the device, keeping things fast and avoiding unnecessary transfers.

Also, the advanced kernels can also access:

- **Shared memory**, which is a small, fast memory region shared among threads in a block, useful for algorithms that need cooperation.
- the **Registers**, which are ultra-fast storage private to each thread.
- And the, **Constant and texture memory**, which are special-purpose spaces for read-only or spatially-coherent data, which we will explore in later chapters.

So, with all this, we now have a complete workflow, something like the below:

- Allocate arrays on the GPU
- Move data from host to device and back
- Write and launch simple kernels
- Observe and manage GPU memory usage

Every project that supports GPU acceleration will follow these steps. As we level up, we will want to keep as much of the computation on the device as possible, and use host-device transfers only for input and final output. With this knowledge, you're all set to take our GPU workflows to the next level.

Simple Vector Addition Kernel

We're about to build our first custom GPU kernel for a basic task, like vector addition. Every new GPU programmer has to do this exercise to be considered part of the team. We're going to take a look at creating, launching, and verifying a kernel that adds two vectors together using both CuPy and PyCUDA. We'll also compare our GPU results with the CPU equivalent to make sure everything's working right.

Installing PyCUDA

We've got CuPy ready, which is great for most high-level GPU array work. If you want even more control and direct access to CUDA C, you can use PyCUDA. It lets us write raw CUDA kernels and gives us a lot of control over memory management, kernel launches, and device contexts, all from Python.

First, let's install PyCUDA in our Python environment.

```
pip install pycuda
```

Once installed, we can import PyCUDA modules and start using its features right away.

Vectors on Host and Device

We will start by setting up our input data using both NumPy (CPU) and CuPy (GPU):

```
import numpy as np
import cupy as cp
# Set vector size
N = 1_000_000
# Create two random input vectors on the host
```

```
a_host = np.random.rand(N).astype(np.float32)
b_host = np.random.rand(N).astype(np.float32)
# Compute CPU result for verification
c_cpu = a_host + b_host
# Transfer input vectors to GPU using CuPy
a_gpu = cp.asarray(a_host)
b_gpu = cp.asarray(b_host)
```

Writing Vector Addition Kernel

Our kernel will receive two arrays (**a** and **b**) and compute their sum elementwise, storing the result in a third array **c**. So here, we will write this kernel as a string in CUDA C:

```
kernel_code = r'''
extern "C" __global__
void vector_add(const float* a, const float* b, float* c, int
n) {
    int idx = blockDim.x * blockIdx.x + threadIdx.x;
    if (idx < n) {
        c[idx] = a[idx] + b[idx];
    }
}
'''
```

Running Kernel with CuPy

The CuPy makes it easy to compile and launch raw CUDA kernels from Python. And to do this, we first have to allocate our output array:

```
c_gpu = cp.empty_like(a_gpu)
threads_per_block = 256
blocks_per_grid = (N + threads_per_block - 1) //
threads_per_block
module = cp.RawModule(code=kernel_code)
```

```
vector_add = module.get_function('vector_add')
vector_add((blocks_per_grid,), (threads_per_block,), (a_gpu,
b_gpu, c_gpu, N))
```

Then we copy the result back to the host and compare with the CPU version:

```
c_result = cp.asnumpy(c_gpu)
print("Are GPU and CPU results equal?", np.allclose(c_result,
c_cpu))
```

After this, we should see **True**. With this, we can now successfully run our first custom kernel with CuPy!

Writing and Running Same Kernel with PyCUDA

Then, we'll dive into PyCUDA to get even more hands-on with the CUDA framework. To start, let's import the modules and sort out our arrays:

```
import pycuda.autoinit
import pycuda.driver as drv
import pycuda.gpuarray as gpuarray
from pycuda.compiler import SourceModule
# Transfer input data to GPU
a_gpu_py = gpuarray.to_gpu(a_host)
b_gpu_py = gpuarray.to_gpu(b_host)
c_gpu_py = gpuarray.empty_like(a_gpu_py)
```

We then compile the kernel and get the function handle:

```
mod = SourceModule(kernel_code)
vector_add_func = mod.get_function("vector_add")
```

After this, we launch the kernel using PyCUDA's syntax:

```
vector_add_func(
    a_gpu_py, b_gpu_py, c_gpu_py, np.int32(N),
    block=(threads_per_block, 1, 1), grid=(blocks_per_grid, 1)
```

```
)
```

Next, we then transfer the result back to the host and check correctness:

```
c_result_py = c_gpu_py.get()
print("PyCUDA GPU result matches CPU?",
np.allclose(c_result_py, c_cpu))
```

Now here, we should again see **`True`**. Both libraries give us the same result, confirming that our kernel works! With this, we can say we have now written, compiled, and launched a custom CUDA kernel in both CuPy and PyCUDA. We have performed elementwise vector addition at lightning speed and verified that the results match our CPU computation. This is the foundation for all further GPU programming as every complex operation is built from these patterns.

Summary

Overall, we've set a solid foundation for practical GPU programming by going through every essential building block in this chapter. We began by learning about the real-world need for high-performance data processing, finding out how traditional CPUs often hit bottlenecks with modern workloads, and understanding why GPUs, with their thousands of lightweight cores, can speed up tasks like machine learning inference and large-scale analytics. We took a look at the Streaming Multiprocessor design, learning how SMs, warps, and occupancy metrics let you run things in parallel efficiently. We also learned about the tricks that allow GPUs to hide memory latency and keep everything busy.

Then, we dove headfirst into mapping multidimensional arrays to CUDA grids and blocks. We mastered the concepts of thread hierarchy, index calculation, and robust boundary handling. We went through the whole GPU data processing workflow in Python, from setting up device memory with CuPy to moving data between the host and device, launching custom kernels, and then copying the results back to validate everything. We tried writing and running our first custom CUDA C kernel with both CuPy and PyCUDA, and we experienced the whole round-trip—from preparing data on the CPU to verifying the GPU output. With these skills and habits, we're all set to dive into more advanced and creative uses of GPU programming throughout the rest of the book.

CHAPTER 2: SETTING UP GPU PROGRAMMING ENVIRONMENT

Installing CUDA Drivers and Toolkit

We've already put our first GPU kernels together using CuPy and PyCUDA, and we've even launched them! Our work so far depended on a development environment set up the right way, but it's important for us to make sure that everything under the hood is correct and will last, especially as we get more into GPU programming and start using more advanced CUDA features.

This chapter's all about double-checking every part of our environment, making sure our system stays stable, reproducible, and good to go with any new library or tool we might want to check out. Even if our earlier code ran smoothly, this is our chance to make sure that our CUDA drivers, toolkit, and environment variables are installed and configured for top performance and flexibility.

Reviewing CUDA Stack

Our ability to run GPU code from Python relies on three layers working in harmony:

- The **NVIDIA driver**, which links the Linux operating system to our GPU hardware.
- The **CUDA toolkit**, which provides command-line tools (like **nvcc**), development libraries, and essential runtime components.
- And, lastly our Python libraries (CuPy, PyCUDA), which use the toolkit to translate our code into high-performance GPU instructions.

We want all these three components to match in version and configuration, making sure we are using the latest features and the most stable drivers for our hardware.

Installing NVIDIA Driver

Before running any heavy GPU workloads, we first confirm our driver is current and compatible with our GPU and CUDA toolkit. Even if our code in Chapter 1 executed without issues, the following helps to verify:

```
nvidia-smi
```

This command reveals our GPU model, installed driver version, and current usage. If the driver needs an update (or was missing), we download the correct package from the *NVIDIA Driver Downloads* page.

Alternarively, we can install it using the package manager as below:

```
sudo apt update
sudo apt install nvidia-driver-535
```

Once the installation completes, a reboot locks in the changes.

Installing CUDA Toolkit

With a working driver, we continue by installing the CUDA toolkit. The toolkit not only enables kernel compilation but also brings in the development headers and sample projects that some Python libraries may reference.

In the below, we check if the toolkit is present:

```
nvcc --version
```

If we see version information, we are set. Otherwise, we download the installer from the *CUDA Toolkit Archive* or through the following package:

```
sudo apt install nvidia-cuda-toolkit
```

During this process, we make a note of the installation directory which is by default, **/usr/local/cuda**.

Setting Environment Variables

We need to be sure our shell session knows where to find the CUDA tools and libraries. This is critical for both command-line usage and for our Python libraries to locate the CUDA runtime.

For this, we add the following lines to our **.bashrc** or **.zshrc**:

```
export PATH=/usr/local/cuda/bin:$PATH
export LD_LIBRARY_PATH=/usr/local/cuda/lib64:$LD_LIBRARY_PATH
```

Next, we then reload the configuration:

```
source ~/.bashrc
```

This confirms that every new terminal session has access to the full CUDA stack.

Now, the validation of our setup is very important and it is just to ensure that nothing goes wrong when we are busy in programming. At first, we verify the toolkit:

```
nvcc --version
```

This shows our toolkit version. Next, we use **nvidia-smi** to confirm our GPU is present and healthy. We can also use CuPy or PyCUDA to programmatically confirm our CUDA runtime:

```
import cupy as cp
print("CuPy version:", cp.__version__)
```

```
print("CUDA runtime version:",
cp.cuda.runtime.runtimeGetVersion())
print("Our available device:", cp.cuda.Device(0).name)
```

If these commands work, we know for certain our hardware and software stack is ready for custom kernels, or even for large-scale machine learning.

With these steps, we have closed the loop between the environment setup in Chapter 1 and the deeper confidence we need for future topics. We are now certain that our Linux system, our NVIDIA GPU, and our Python tools are tightly integrated, robust, and ready for any project we want to build.

Verifying GPU with Device Query

We've installed the CUDA drivers and toolkit, and confirmed that our system sees the GPU. Before we get into more detail, let's take a closer look at the hardware in our machine. Device queries let us see every important detail about our GPU, like how many multiprocessors it has, the available memory, supported compute capability, and other features that affect our CUDA programming.

When you run a device query, it shows that your installation was successful and helps us adjust our kernels and library settings to match your hardware. This makes our programming more robust, predictable, and performant as we move forward.

Running Device Query

The CUDA toolkit comes with a handy sample binary called **deviceQuery**. This tool prints a full report on every visible GPU in our system.

On most of the Linux setups, we find **deviceQuery** at:

/usr/local/cuda/samples/1_Utilities/deviceQuery/deviceQuery

If we do not see it, we can build the CUDA samples directory as below:

```
cd /usr/local/cuda/samples/1_Utilities/deviceQuery
sudo make
./deviceQuery
```

The output displays a long list of properties, and in them some of the most useful lines for us are:

- Device Name
- Total Global Memory

- Multiprocessors Count
- CUDA Cores per SM
- Maximum Threads per Block
- Shared Memory per Block
- Compute Capability

Verifying Device Properties

We often want to access these settings directly in Python, especially if our code needs to adapt to different hardware. With CuPy, we can programmatically inspect everything we need.

Now, we'll print out the most important properties:

```
import cupy as cp

device = cp.cuda.Device(0)

attributes = device.attributes

print("Device Name:", device.name)

print("Compute Capability:",
f"{attributes['ComputeCapabilityMajor']}.{attributes['ComputeC
apabilityMinor']}")

print("Total Global Memory (MB):", device.mem_info[1] // (1024
* 1024))

print("Multiprocessors:", attributes['MultiProcessorCount'])

print("Max Threads per Block:",
attributes['MaxThreadsPerBlock'])

print("Shared Memory per Block (KB):",
attributes['MaxSharedMemoryPerBlock'] // 1024)
```

We see every property that will impact our code: how big we can make our thread blocks, how much memory we can allocate, and what features are supported.

Validating Compute Capability

The **compute capability** tells us what generation of CUDA features our GPU supports. For example, 6.x, 7.x, or 8.x refers to "Pascal," "Volta," "Turing," "Ampere," and newer architectures. Each bump in compute capability unlocks new instructions, more shared memory, and new acceleration features.

Most modern CUDA libraries require compute capability 6.0 or above. If our GPU reports 7.5, 8.6, or similar, we are ready for nearly every current CUDA library, including the latest versions of CuPy, PyCUDA, and deep learning frameworks. If our device reports very low compute capability (like 3.x or below), some features may not be available. In that case, we would either limit our use to compatible libraries or consider a hardware upgrade.

We can also query device properties in PyCUDA:

```
import pycuda.driver as drv
import pycuda.autoinit
device = drv.Device(0)
print("Device Name:", device.name())
print("Compute Capability:",
f"{device.compute_capability()[0]}.{device.compute_capability(
)[1]}")
print("Total Global Memory (MB):", device.total_memory() //
(1024 * 1024))
for key, value in device.get_attributes().items():
    print(f"{key}: {value}")
```

This shows us all available properties, so we can adapt our kernel configuration as needed.

Whenever we change machines, GPUs, or drivers, running a fresh device query should always be our first step to validate compatibility. With this practice, our CUDA programming remains reliable, flexible, and perfectly matched to the hardware at hand.

Implementing Kernel in PyCUDA

We've already written a basic vector addition kernel using PyCUDA, but now we want to learn more about how PyCUDA lets us put and run custom CUDA C code in our Python scripts. We want to get comfortable with the whole host-device workflow: allocating memory, moving data, writing a more flexible kernel, compiling it on the fly, launching it, and then retrieving and validating results.

This example is better than our previous one. Here, we'll be talking about parameterization, trying out new operations, and making it clear why PyCUDA is such a solid bridge between Python and the CUDA ecosystem.

Preparing Host Data

We will start by setting up two input arrays and a placeholder for output. We will begin to make use of NumPy on the host for easy setup.

```
import numpy as np
N = 8
a_host = np.arange(N, dtype=np.float32)
b_host = np.arange(N, 0, -1).astype(np.float32)
print("Input Array A:", a_host)
print("Input Array B:", b_host)
```

We choose small arrays for clarity, but the same workflow applies for much larger datasets.

Allocating Device Memory

With PyCUDA, we transfer these arrays to the GPU. We also allocate space for our result.

```
import pycuda.autoinit
import pycuda.driver as drv
import pycuda.gpuarray as gpuarray
a_device = gpuarray.to_gpu(a_host)
b_device = gpuarray.to_gpu(b_host)
c_device = gpuarray.empty_like(a_device)
```

At this point, **`a_device`** and **`b_device`** are on the GPU, and **`c_device`** is reserved space for our results.

Writing Custom CUDA C Kernel

This is where PyCUDA shines. We can embed CUDA C code as a string and compile it at runtime. By doing this, our kernel will add two arrays elementwise, but we can also change the operation easily.

Following is the CUDA C script:

```
from pycuda.compiler import SourceModule
kernel_code = """
__global__ void add_arrays(float *a, float *b, float *c, int
n)
{
    int idx = threadIdx.x + blockDim.x * blockIdx.x;
```

```
    if (idx < n)
    {
        c[idx] = a[idx] + b[idx];  // Try changing this
operation!
    }
}
"""
mod = SourceModule(kernel_code)
add_arrays = mod.get_function("add_arrays")
```

The CUDA requires us to specify how many threads to run in each block, and how many blocks to launch. For simplicity, we can use a block size of 4 and calculate the grid size to cover all elements.

```
threads_per_block = 4
blocks_per_grid = (N + threads_per_block - 1) //
threads_per_block
```

Launching Kernel and Validating Results

We then call our kernel using PyCUDA's function interface. All pointers and parameters are passed in the order they appear in our kernel.

```
add_arrays(
    a_device, b_device, c_device, np.int32(N),
    block=(threads_per_block, 1, 1), grid=(blocks_per_grid, 1)
)
```

The kernel runs asynchronously on the GPU, processing all elements in parallel.

After the computation, we copy our result from the GPU back to the host and validate against the CPU calculation.

```
c_host = c_device.get()
print("Result Array C:", c_host)
# Validate correctness
```

```
expected = a_host + b_host
if np.allclose(c_host, expected):
    print("Result matches CPU computation.")
else:
    print("Mismatch found!")
```

To quickly summarize what we did:

- We first allocate device arrays only as large as we need—no need to worry about host RAM.
- The PyCUDA automatically handles host-to-device and device-to-host movement when using **`to_gpu()`** and **`.get()`**.
- Our CUDA C code is embedded and compiled the moment our script runs, letting us iterate quickly.
- We then control block and grid sizes, gaining flexibility for any problem size or complexity.
- And then finally, by checking results against a CPU version, we catch mistakes early and build confidence in our GPU programming skills.

This gives us a reliable, flexible pattern for embedding and validating CUDA C kernels in our Python projects using PyCUDA. This is a really useful skill that'll be key for when we move on to more challenging and creative GPU programming tasks.

Managing Python Virtual Environments

Why Virtual Environments Matter?

Since we're expanding our GPU programming toolkit, our Python projects are starting to rely on a growing collection of libraries—like CuPy, PyCUDA, NumPy, and many others. Each of these might need specific versions, and those requirements can change from project to project or even from one tutorial to the next. If you don't keep an eye on it, our global Python installation can quickly become a tangled mess, leading to version conflicts and broken dependencies. That's where virtual environments come in handy.

A virtual environment lets us set up a self-contained Python workspace, separate from the rest of the system. In this workspace, we install the exact libraries and versions we want. This isolation makes it so we can reproduce our results, share our environment with others, and avoid accidental upgrades or conflicts when we install new packages. We can also experiment and break things without risking our global setup.

Creating Virtual Environment

Conda is one of the most popular tools for managing Python environments, especially in the data science and GPU computing world. It works on Linux, macOS, and Windows, and offers prebuilt binaries for many GPU libraries.

We will create a new environment dedicated to our GPU projects:

```
conda create -n mygpu python=3.10
```

This command creates an environment called **mygpu** with Python 3.10. We can use any name and Python version we prefer.

Now, to activate our new environment, we then type:

```
conda activate mygpu
```

After this, we are now working inside an isolated workspace. Any libraries we install here won't affect the rest of our system.

Installing GPU Libraries

With our environment active, we can install CuPy, PyCUDA, and other essentials. The Conda often provides optimized builds for CUDA:

```
conda install -c conda-forge cupy pycuda
```

This pulls in compatible versions for our CUDA toolkit automatically. If we want more control, or if a package isn't available via conda, we can still use pip within this environment:

```
pip install <library-name>
```

All of the packages installed this way remain within the virtual environment. To check which packages are installed and their versions, run:

```
conda list
```

Keeping Projects Reproducible

To save and share our environment, we can export its specifications:

```
conda env export > environment.yml
```

Anyone with this file can reproduce our environment exactly:

```
conda env create -f environment.yml
```

This is especially valuable for team projects, sharing tutorials, or moving code between machines.

By building our workflow inside a designated conda environment, we ensure that our projects are robust, reproducible, and easy to maintain. This practice is going to help us a lot in the long run with GPU programming and any complex Python work we take on next.

Summary

To sum up we have successfully established a reliable and professional-grade environment for GPU programming, ensuring that every step of our workflow remains robust, reproducible, and tailored to our needs. We began by reinforcing our understanding of the relationship between CUDA drivers, the CUDA toolkit, and our NVIDIA hardware, making certain all pieces are aligned for maximum performance. We learned to install and validate the toolkit and drivers, update our environment variables, and use built-in tools such as **`nvidia-smi`** and **`nvcc`** to verify the system's readiness for heavy GPU workloads.

By running the CUDA device query and inspecting our GPU properties, both from the command line and within Python, we gained insight into our device's compute capability, available memory, and architectural limits. This empowers us to tune our code and library choices to best fit our hardware. Through hands-on work with PyCUDA, we practiced embedding, compiling, and executing CUDA C kernels from Python, reinforcing every aspect of the host–device workflow. Finally, we set up conda-based virtual environments, learned to isolate dependencies, and created fully reproducible workspaces. This not only prevents conflicts but also makes our projects easier to share, maintain, and expand.

Chapter 3: Basic Data Transfers and Memory Types

Host and Device Memory Regions

Understanding Host and Device Memory Spaces

Every GPU project we start has one thing in common: our data can live in two completely different places, host memory and device memory. Host memory is basically the main RAM of your computer, where all the standard Python data structures, NumPy arrays, and operating system processes run. The CPU and most of the traditional Python code can access this memory. Device memory, on the other hand, is located on the GPU itself. It's sometimes called VRAM or global memory, and it's only accessible to the GPU's many cores during the execution of CUDA kernels or device-side operations. This physical separation is actually more important than it seems at first. Our CPU can't access or edit data stored in device memory without first copying it back to host memory. The GPU can't work directly with data in our computer's main RAM either. It needs us to transfer the data to the GPU's memory first. Whenever we design a GPU-accelerated workflow, we should always keep the following in mind: Where's my data now, and where should it be for my next operation?

As we create more complex GPU workflows, we understand that managing this difference is key for performance and accuracy. Each memory region has its own strengths. Host memory lets you interact with the CPU seamlessly, so it's great for serial or I/O-bound tasks. Device memory lets you do parallel, high-throughput computation at scales the CPU can't match.

Exploring Allocation Methods

It's important to choose an allocation method that works well for you, because it'll determine where your arrays are stored and how you interact with them. The process starts on the host using NumPy or standard Python tools:

```
import numpy as np
host_array = np.arange(1_000_000, dtype=np.float32)
```

This creates an array entirely in system RAM. We can pass this array to CPU functions and manipulate it with all the tools Python offers. However, the GPU remains unaware of this array's existence until we explicitly move it.

To allocate an array in device memory, we turn to CuPy or PyCUDA. With CuPy, the process mirrors what we know from NumPy:

```
import cupy as cp
device_array = cp.zeros(1_000_000, dtype=cp.float32)
```

The allocation happens on the GPU, with no copy to or from the host unless we request it. We can now apply GPU kernels to this array and leverage thousands of parallel threads.

The PyCUDA provides its own GPUArray object, which functions much like CuPy arrays:

```
import pycuda.autoinit
import pycuda.gpuarray as gpuarray
device_array_py = gpuarray.zeros(1_000_000, dtype=np.float32)
```

Again, this allocation occurs directly on the device. No host-side memory is touched unless we perform an explicit copy. If we begin with data on the host, we must transfer it to the device before launching a kernel. If we allocate on the device, we can keep the data there for the duration of all GPU-based operations, only moving it back to the host if we need to save or inspect the results.

Recognizing Differences in Access Patterns

Both the CPU and GPU memory are designed for very different usage patterns. The CPU is great at accessing random memory locations and has deep hardware caches and a strong prefetcher to help it out. The GPU gets its performance from high-bandwidth, bulk access, especially when a lot of threads work together to read blocks of memory that are next to each other. When we process arrays on the GPU, we've got to think about how threads access device memory. If you get accesses across threads in a warp to be adjacent and lined up, you'll get the most out of the memory controller. That way, you can do things like coalesced loads and stores. If the access patterns are all over the place, it'll slow things down because the GPU has to fetch multiple cache lines for a single operation.

And transfers between the host and device memory need some planning too. Copying large blocks of data is way more efficient than moving a bunch of small arrays one by one. So, we try to batch our transfers: moving whole arrays at once and doing all we can with the GPU before copying the results back to the host. There's some overlap between memory operations and computation, especially with advanced features like CUDA streams or pinned memory. This keeps the GPU busy while the data is still moving, which makes the performance higher in multi-stage processing pipelines.

Performance Implications in Workflows

The line between the host and the device's memory can really affect how well things perform. Every time you transfer data between these two spaces, it takes a certain amount of time, and this cost gets more expensive as the data gets bigger. A single transfer of a million floats might take only a fraction of a second, but if it's repeated many times per second, this overhead quickly dominates the runtime of our application.

We've also got to think about the real world impact of not having enough memory on the GPU. Modern GPUs have way less device memory than our system RAM—often 8GB to 24GB, compared to 32GB, 64GB, or more on the host. This means we've got to plan which data is on the GPU at any given moment, especially for workflows involving very large datasets. We divide our data into chunks and process it in batches so we don't exceed the available device memory.

Also, if you're careful with your memory management, you can avoid losing or corrupting data by accident. If you try to run a kernel on data that's still in the host memory, you'll probably get errors or incorrect results. Also, if you try to process a NumPy array directly with GPU functions, you'll get exceptions. These bugs are often hard to spot, so it's best to keep an eye on where our data is stored and make sure to move arrays to the right memory region before launching operations.

Sample WorkFlow: Transfers Between Host and Device

We will walk through a common sequence: preparing data on the host, transferring it to the device, processing it with a kernel, and copying the results back to the host.

First, we create and fill our data using NumPy:

```
import numpy as np
host_input = np.random.rand(1_000_000).astype(np.float32)
```

Next, we transfer this array to device memory using CuPy:

```
import cupy as cp
device_input = cp.asarray(host_input)
```

Processing happens entirely on the device:

```
device_output = cp.sqrt(device_input)
```

Finally, we transfer the result back to the host for use in further Python processing or for saving to disk:

```
host_output = cp.asnumpy(device_output)
```

This workflow is key to any GPU-accelerated project. We put all our transfers together and do all the heavy lifting on the device to make the most of the performance and save as much overhead as possible.

Advanced Memory Types

But as we get more familiar with GPU programming, we find that CUDA has a bunch of different memory types to make transfers and computations faster and more efficient.

- **Pinned (page-locked) memory** allows faster transfers by ensuring the data sits in a fixed location in host RAM, reducing the overhead of moving it to the device.

- **Unified memory** provides a shared address space, letting the CUDA runtime move data between host and device as needed, simplifying programming at the cost of some performance control.
- **Zero-copy memory** enables the GPU to directly access host memory, useful for certain streaming workflows or when device memory is limited.

For most projects, understanding host and device memory suffices. However, these advanced types unlock new possibilities and further efficiency for specialized use cases. Every subsequent topic in this chapter builds on this foundation, giving us the skills to manage memory, optimize transfers, and create workflows that take full advantage of both our CPU and GPU.

Synchronous vs. Asynchronous Copies

Definitions

We often think of data transfer between host and device as a single, simple action. In reality, we have two distinct modes of transfer: synchronous and asynchronous. Understanding these modes is vital for high-performance GPU programming because the way we schedule and execute transfers affects not only speed but also how efficiently our code uses both CPU and GPU resources.

A **synchronous transfer** means our Python script will wait until the data movement has finished before moving on to the next operation. In this case, the copy command "blocks" all further code execution until every byte of data has reached its destination. For small or occasional transfers, this blocking may be barely noticeable. However, when we work with large arrays or when transfers happen frequently, synchronous copying can slow down our entire workflow, keeping our CPU idle while waiting for the transfer to finish.

An **asynchronous transfer** works differently. Instead of waiting for the operation to complete, our code schedules the transfer and then moves forward immediately. The GPU and its driver take care of actually moving the data in the background, while our script is free to do something else—perhaps launch another kernel, prepare more data, or even start additional transfers. Asynchronous copies allow us to overlap communication and computation, hiding transfer latency and letting us squeeze the maximum throughput out of our hardware.

Performance Impact

The distinction between synchronous and asynchronous copies may seem minor, but it has huge implications for performance in real-world workloads. When we rely on synchronous transfers, the CPU and GPU often sit idle, waiting for each other to finish a task. This underutilization limits how much work we can do per second, especially when large data batches need to move between host and device repeatedly.

When we switch to asynchronous copies, we can queue up a bunch of operations. The driver and

GPU execute them as resources become available, effectively building a pipeline. This means our CPU prepares the next workload or processes results while the GPU is busy transferring or computing, maximizing both sides' efficiency. When used the right way, asynchronous transfers can almost double effective throughput in some workflows, especially when they're used with streaming and batch processing.

Synchronous and Asynchronous Methods in CuPy

The CuPy provides clear and accessible ways to handle both types of transfers. The default methods like **cp.asarray()** and **cp.asnumpy()** are synchronous. This means when we write:

```
import numpy as np
import cupy as cp
host_data = np.random.rand(100_000_000).astype(np.float32)
device_data = cp.asarray(host_data)
```

Our Python process halts at the **cp.asarray()** call, and the line does not return until every value has landed safely in device memory. This guarantees that, when the next operation starts, all the data is ready for GPU computation. The same behavior applies when moving results from device back to host.

If we want to unlock the power of asynchronous transfers, we use CuPy's **cp.cuda.Stream()** objects. By creating a stream and passing it to copy functions, we schedule the transfer to run in the background as shown in the below:

```
stream = cp.cuda.Stream(non_blocking=True)
with stream:
    device_data_async = cp.asarray(host_data)
# Our script continues, even while the transfer runs in the
background
```

The operations inside the stream context are queued on the stream and, as long as there are no explicit synchronizations, our Python code moves forward. If we want to make sure all queued operations in a stream are finished before using the data, we call:

```
stream.synchronize()
```

This manual synchronization allows us to decide the optimal moment to wait for results, giving us fine-grained control over the flow of execution.

Sample Program: Blocking Behavior and Queue Management

We will see this difference in a short program shown below. We will measure the time it takes to copy a large array from host to device, first using the synchronous method, and then using asynchronous transfers with explicit stream management.

```
import time
import numpy as np
import cupy as cp
host_data = np.random.rand(200_000_000).astype(np.float32)
start = time.time()
device_data = cp.asarray(host_data)
end = time.time()
print("Synchronous transfer time (seconds):", end - start)
```

Now here, we notice that our code pauses until the transfer is complete. For very large arrays, this delay becomes substantial.

In the below, we then try the asynchronous transfer using the CuPy streams:

```
import time
host_data = np.random.rand(200_000_000).astype(np.float32)
stream = cp.cuda.Stream(non_blocking=True)
start = time.time()
with stream:
    device_data_async = cp.asarray(host_data)
    # Other work could go here
# Wait for transfer to complete before using the data
stream.synchronize()
end = time.time()
print("Asynchronous transfer time (seconds):", end - start)
```

If we add more computation or kernel launches between the start and the synchronization, we often observe a net speedup. The transfer and computation can run in parallel, taking full advantage of hardware concurrency.

When to Use?

In my experience, synchronous transfers are great for simple scripts, quick prototyping, or when we only need to transfer small arrays every now and then. They're simple and easy to understand, making sure our data is always ready for the next step. But as our programs get more complex or bigger, asynchronous transfers become super important. In batch processing, deep learning pipelines, or any scenario where data moves between host and device all the time, asynchronous copies help keep CPU and GPU busy, reducing wait times and boosting performance. Plus, with streams, you get even more precise control over your queue management. We can assign specific streams to different tasks, overlap multiple transfers and kernels, or carefully order operations to avoid contention.

The choice between synchronous and asynchronous depends on our workflow's size, complexity, and need for maximal efficiency. By understanding and applying both approaches, we gain flexibility and power in every GPU programming project, moving confidently between simple scripts and high-performance pipelines.

Pinned Memory for Faster Transfers

Why Host Memory Matters for Transfers?

Whenever we move data between the host or the CPU and the device or the GPU, the underlying type of host memory can have a huge effect on transfer speed. By default, our arrays in NumPy or Python reside in regular "pageable" memory. This memory can be swapped in and out by the operating system, which provides flexibility for the system overall but introduces overhead for direct device access. When the GPU requests data from pageable memory, the system has to make an extra copy to a temporary, fixed-location buffer before starting the actual transfer. This extra step slows down the whole process, especially for large arrays.

The pinned (also called "page-locked") memory gives us a major speed boost. When we allocate pinned memory, we instruct the operating system to keep that memory region in physical RAM and never move it to disk. This lets the GPU DMA engine (direct memory access) transfer data straight from RAM to the device without any temporary copy. As a result, we see a measurable increase in bandwidth for both small and large transfers. For many high-throughput GPU applications, using pinned memory is a practical way to accelerate host–device communication.

Allocating Pinned Memory

The CuPy makes it easy for us to allocate pinned memory. Instead of creating a NumPy array as usual, we use CuPy's pinned memory pool as shown below:

```
import cupy as cp
```

```
# Allocate a pinned host array
pinned_pool = cp.cuda.PinnedMemoryPool()
cp.cuda.set_pinned_memory_allocator(pinned_pool.malloc)
size = 100_000_000
pinned_host = cp.ndarray((size,), dtype=cp.float32,
memptr=pinned_pool.malloc(size *
cp.dtype(cp.float32).itemsize))
```

This above array looks and behaves like any CuPy array, but it resides in a region of RAM that the GPU can access much more efficiently. When we use this array for transfers, we get the benefits of zero-copy access on supported hardware or, at minimum, reduced latency and increased bandwidth for host–device movement.

Pinned vs. Pageable Memory

Now let us try to see how we can really look at appreciating the difference between these memories. We will try to measure the transfer speeds for both pageable (regular NumPy) memory and pinned memory. To do this, we will set up two arrays of equal size; one regular, one pinned, and then we will time their transfer to the GPU.

Following is the example:

```
import cupy as cp
import numpy as np
import time
size = 100_000_000
# Regular pageable host array (NumPy)
pageable_host = np.random.rand(size).astype(np.float32)
# Pinned host array (CuPy)
pinned_pool = cp.cuda.PinnedMemoryPool()
cp.cuda.set_pinned_memory_allocator(pinned_pool.malloc)
pinned_host = cp.ndarray((size,), dtype=cp.float32,
memptr=pinned_pool.malloc(size *
cp.dtype(cp.float32).itemsize))
pinned_host[:] = pageable_host  # Copy data into pinned array
# Time transfer from pageable memory
```

```
start_pageable = time.time()
device_array_pageable = cp.asarray(pageable_host)
cp.cuda.Stream.null.synchronize()
end_pageable = time.time()
print("Transfer time (pageable):", end_pageable -
start_pageable, "seconds")
# Time transfer from pinned memory
start_pinned = time.time()
device_array_pinned = cp.asarray(pinned_host)
cp.cuda.Stream.null.synchronize()
end_pinned = time.time()
print("Transfer time (pinned):", end_pinned - start_pinned,
"seconds")
```

As we can see in the above, we synchronize after each transfer to ensure that timing only includes the data movement, not queued operations. On most systems, we see that transfers from pinned memory complete noticeably faster, particularly as the array size increases.

Overall, the pinned memory makes the most sense when we have large, frequent transfers or when low latency is critical, such as in streaming, real-time data processing, or machine learning workloads that must move batches of data quickly. For simple scripts or experiments, regular memory is usually fine and keeps the code portable. When we aim to maximize bandwidth or build high-throughput systems, adding pinned memory to our workflow unlocks an extra level of speed.

Using Unified Memory with CuPy

Simplifies Workflow

After doing a bit of GPU programming, we've learned a few things. It's really important to know where your data is—on the host or on the device—and how much attention you need to pay to data transfers. So, up to this point, every time we wanted to process data on the GPU, we moved it explicitly from host memory to device memory. And we moved it back if we wanted to see the results in Python. While this clear-cut approach gives us great control and top performance, it can sometimes make our code more complicated and less flexible, especially when our algorithms move dynamically between CPU and GPU, or when we're prototyping new workflows.

The unified memory, introduced with CUDA's **cudaMallocManaged**, changes the game. With unified memory, we allocate a single memory region that both the CPU and GPU can access directly. The CUDA driver and runtime take care of migrating data between host and device as needed. This means we can write code that manipulates our data from either side, without worrying about explicit copies or maintaining separate host/device arrays. Unified memory is especially useful for rapid prototyping, algorithms that switch back and forth between CPU and GPU, and for cases where the data access pattern is unpredictable at runtime. When we use unified memory, we allocate and work with one array—no need to think about moving data. If the CPU accesses the array, the CUDA runtime makes sure it's available in RAM; if a GPU kernel accesses it, the runtime migrates it to device memory. We focus on writing our algorithms, and CUDA handles the logistics. While explicit transfers remain fastest for critical code paths, unified memory can greatly reduce programming effort, prevent bugs, and even allow our programs to work on data sizes that don't fit fully in GPU memory (the system transparently pages' data as needed).

When to Use Unified Memory?

The unified memory is ideal for:

- Rapid development and testing, when minimizing code complexity matters.
- Algorithms that switch frequently between CPU and GPU.
- Multi-GPU or multi-process workloads where explicit memory management is challenging.
- Situations where data sizes might exceed device memory.

For fine-tuned, performance-critical paths, we can always combine unified memory with explicit transfers or optimize with pinned memory, as needed.

Sample Program: Vector Addition with Unified Memory

The CuPy supports unified memory with the **mem_alloc_managed** function, which lets us allocate a managed memory buffer accessible by both host and device. Although not every function in CuPy uses unified memory by default, we can allocate unified arrays and launch kernels that work directly on this memory.

In the following, we will step through a vector addition example using unified memory. At first, we allocate unified memory for our arrays using CuPy's managed allocation function:

```
import cupy as cp

import numpy as np

size = 1_000_000

# Allocate unified memory arrays for input and output

a_managed = cp.cuda.memory.alloc_managed(size *
cp.dtype(cp.float32).itemsize)
```

```
b_managed = cp.cuda.memory.alloc_managed(size *
cp.dtype(cp.float32).itemsize)
c_managed = cp.cuda.memory.alloc_managed(size *
cp.dtype(cp.float32).itemsize)
```

We now have three buffers, each in unified memory. We can access these from both CPU and GPU. Next, we can then treat these buffers as NumPy arrays using Python's buffer interface:

```
# Map managed memory as NumPy arrays (host access)
a_host = np.frombuffer(a_managed, dtype=np.float32,
count=size)
b_host = np.frombuffer(b_managed, dtype=np.float32,
count=size)
c_host = np.frombuffer(c_managed, dtype=np.float32,
count=size)
a_host[:] = np.random.rand(size).astype(np.float32)
b_host[:] = np.random.rand(size).astype(np.float32)
```

At this stage, our data is ready, and no explicit host-to-device transfer is needed.

Writing and Launching Kernel

Now here, we write a simple CUDA kernel for vector addition, just as before:

```
kernel_code = r'''
extern "C" __global__
void vec_add(const float* a, const float* b, float* c, int n)
{
    int idx = blockDim.x * blockIdx.x + threadIdx.x;
    if (idx < n) {
        c[idx] = a[idx] + b[idx];
    }
}
'''
module = cp.RawModule(code=kernel_code)
```

```
vec_add = module.get_function('vec_add')
threads_per_block = 256
blocks_per_grid = (size + threads_per_block - 1) //
threads_per_block
vec_add((blocks_per_grid,), (threads_per_block,), (a_managed,
b_managed, c_managed, size))
```

The kernel reads **a_managed** and **b_managed**, performs the addition, and writes the result into **c_managed**—all without us needing to do any memory transfers.

Validating Host Results

Once the kernel has completed, you'll have instant access to your results on the CPU since unified memory is accessible from both the host and device. We just use NumPy to check the accuracy as shown below:

```
# Validate GPU result using CPU calculation
expected = a_host + b_host
if np.allclose(c_host, expected):
    print("Unified memory vector addition succeeded and is
correct.")
else:
    print("Mismatch detected.")
```

The unified memory greatly simplifies code, but the CUDA runtime still needs to migrate data as needed. For workflows that repeatedly bounce between CPU and GPU access, some overhead may appear compared to explicit, hand-optimized transfers. However, for many real-world problems, especially during development, rapid prototyping, or mixed workloads, the unified memory can bring clarity and convenience with only a modest cost.

If we work with very large datasets, unified memory's automatic paging lets us operate on arrays larger than the GPU's memory. CUDA will page data in and out, making our program robust even in constrained environments.

Overlapping Data Transfer and Compute

Overlaps and CUDA Streams

By default, the transfers and computations often happen one after the other. Generally, we copy data to the GPU, wait for the copy to finish, launch a kernel, and then wait for that kernel to finish before moving the next chunk. This approach leaves the GPU or CPU idle during large parts of the cycle, underutilizing the hardware. When data transfers and kernel execution overlap, meaning data is moving to or from the device at the same time other kernels are running, it helps keep every resource busy and reduces end-to-end latency.

The CUDA streams are the key to achieving this overlap. The streams allow us to schedule work in independent queues, letting transfers and computations run in parallel as much as the hardware allows. A CUDA stream is essentially a command queue for the GPU. Operations placed in different streams can execute concurrently, if resources are available. When we use the default stream (also called the "null" stream), everything runs in order. By assigning transfers and kernels to separate streams, we give the GPU permission to overlap data movement and computation.

To see this in action, we create multiple data buffers—one being transferred while another is being processed. This double-buffering approach is widely used in high-performance GPU workloads to maximize throughput.

Sample Program: Overlapping Transfers and CuPy Compute

We will build a program that demonstrates overlapping by using two CUDA streams. We will transfer a large batch of data to the device in one stream, while a previous batch is processed by the GPU in another stream.

```
import cupy as cp
import numpy as np
import time
# Set problem size and batch parameters
total_size = 100_000_000
batch_size = 10_000_000
# Generate data batches on the host
host_batches = [
    np.random.rand(batch_size).astype(np.float32)
    for _ in range(total_size // batch_size)
]
# Simple kernel: elementwise multiplication
kernel_code = r'''
extern "C" __global__
```

```
void scale(float *a, float scale, int n) {
    int idx = blockDim.x * blockIdx.x + threadIdx.x;
    if (idx < n) {
        a[idx] *= scale;
    }
}
'''
mod = cp.RawModule(code=kernel_code)
scale_kernel = mod.get_function('scale')
threads_per_block = 256
blocks_per_grid = (batch_size + threads_per_block - 1) //
threads_per_block
# Create two streams for overlap
stream_transfer = cp.cuda.Stream(non_blocking=True)
stream_compute = cp.cuda.Stream(non_blocking=True)
results = []
start = time.time()
for i, batch in enumerate(host_batches):
    # Allocate device buffer in transfer stream
    with stream_transfer:
        device_batch = cp.asarray(batch)
    # Wait for transfer to complete before launching compute
in compute stream
    stream_transfer.synchronize()
    with stream_compute:
        scale_kernel(
            (blocks_per_grid,), (threads_per_block,),
            (device_batch, np.float32(1.5), batch_size)
        )
```

```
        # Copy result back asynchronously
        result_host = cp.asnumpy(device_batch)
    stream_compute.synchronize()  # Ensure compute and copy
complete before moving on
    results.append(result_host)
end = time.time()
print(f"Total time for processing with overlap: {end -
start:.2f} seconds")
```

I'll give you the lowdown on where we're at:

- We create two CUDA streams—one dedicated to transfers, one to computation.
- For each batch, we transfer data to the device in the transfer stream.
- Once transfer finishes, we launch the compute kernel and retrieve the results using the compute stream.
- Synchronizations ensure each stage completes before proceeding, but since the next transfer can begin as soon as the compute stream is running, later iterations will see the overlap.

Measuring Bandwidth and Latency

To see the advantage, try running a version where both transfers and kernels use only the default stream, no overlap:

```
start_sync = time.time()
for batch in host_batches:
    device_batch = cp.asarray(batch)
    scale_kernel(
        (blocks_per_grid,), (threads_per_block,),
        (device_batch, np.float32(1.5), batch_size)
    )
    result_host = cp.asnumpy(device_batch)
end_sync = time.time()
print(f"Total time with synchronous (no overlap): {end_sync -
start_sync:.2f} seconds")
```

In real workloads, the overlapping will often reduce total time and help us keep up with streaming input. If you overlap data transfer and computation using CUDA streams, you can unlock the full potential of the GPU's concurrency. This lets us process incoming data continuously, maximize both latency and bandwidth metrics, and build pipelines that really take advantage of all available resources.

Simple Bandwidth Measurement

For efficient GPU workflows, it's vital to understand how fast we can move data between the host and device. No matter how fast your GPU is, it's not going to do much if it's just sitting there waiting for data from the CPU. We can measure the bandwidth of our system—how fast we can transfer data between the host and device. This gives us a good idea of where bottlenecks might show up and how close we are to hitting the limits of our hardware. This insight helps us figure out the size of our arrays, pick the best batch sizes, and know when to think about more advanced stuff like pinned memory or overlapping transfers.

Designing Basic Bandwidth Benchmark

Our goal is to create a script that sends arrays of different sizes from the host to the device and back, times the transfer, and then calculates the effective throughput in gigabytes per second (GB/s). This experiment can be done with both regular (pageable) and pinned memory, but we will start with the simplest setup. We use synchronous transfers and NumPy/CuPy for the core measurement.

Following is a quick script that measures the bandwidth for various array sizes:

```
import numpy as np
import cupy as cp
import time
sizes = [2**10, 2**14, 2**18, 2**20, 2**22, 2**24, 2**26]  #
Array sizes from 1 KB to 64 MB
dtype = np.float32
print(f"{'Array Size (MB)':>15} | {'Host→Device GB/s':>18} |
{'Device→Host GB/s':>18}")
for size in sizes:
    arr = np.random.rand(size).astype(dtype)
    arr_bytes = arr.nbytes / (1024 * 1024)

    # Host to Device
```

```
    start_htod = time.time()
    d_arr = cp.asarray(arr)
    cp.cuda.Stream.null.synchronize()
    end_htod = time.time()
    htod_time = end_htod - start_htod
    htod_gbs = arr.nbytes / (htod_time * 1e9)

    # Device to Host
    start_dtoh = time.time()
    arr2 = cp.asnumpy(d_arr)
    cp.cuda.Stream.null.synchronize()
    end_dtoh = time.time()
    dtoh_time = end_dtoh - start_dtoh
    dtoh_gbs = arr.nbytes / (dtoh_time * 1e9)

    print(f"{arr_bytes:15.2f} | {htod_gbs:18.2f} |
{dtoh_gbs:18.2f}")
```

We will break down the above bandwidth script:

- We select a series of array sizes, doubling each time.
- For each size, we create a random NumPy array and note its size in megabytes.
- We measure the time to transfer from host to device using **cp.asarray()** and then from device back to host using **cp.asnumpy()**, synchronizing after each operation.
- Effective bandwidth is calculated as the array size divided by the transfer time, reported in GB/s.

Results Interpretation

We typically observe that bandwidth increases with larger array sizes. The small arrays don't saturate the bus due to setup overhead, while large arrays approach the hardware's theoretical limits. For most modern GPUs on PCIe Gen3 or Gen4, peak bandwidth for large transfers typically ranges between 8 and 20 GB/s, depending on the exact hardware and whether pinned memory is used.

If we want to explore further, we can rerun the benchmark using pinned memory for the host arrays (as described in an earlier topic). This often increases observed bandwidth, especially for large transfers. We can also repeat the test for device-to-device (GPU-to-GPU) copies if our system supports multiple GPUs, or add asynchronous transfer measurements using CUDA streams to see how concurrency impacts bandwidth.

Summary

With this, we've got a pretty good idea of how memory management and data transfers work. First, we figured out the differences between the host memory and the device memory. Then, we learned how each one is used and how important it is to move the data around so that the GPU can do its thing. We checked out different ways to allocate memory and saw how the way people access things and planning can have a big impact on performance. We figured out the difference between synchronous and asynchronous copies by comparing how they act. We saw that asynchronous transfers, when used with streams, let us overlap data movement and computation for higher throughput.

We tried out pinned memory, and it actually ended up being a pretty useful tool for optimization. It boosts the bandwidth a lot, especially when dealing with large arrays, and it reduces bottlenecks that could slow down even the fastest GPUs. We then figured out how to use CUDA streams to mix up data transfers and kernel execution, boosting both latency and bandwidth in streaming and real-time apps. We finally used some simple but effective benchmarking scripts to measure bandwidth. This gave us the tools we needed to evaluate and optimize data movement on any system.

CHAPTER 4: SIMPLE PARALLEL PATTERNS

Elementwise Operations on Arrays

Elementwise Computation and CuPy

In parallel programming, the most common and straightforward pattern is the elementwise operation. In a lot of real-world problems, we need to apply the same arithmetic operation—addition, subtraction, multiplication, division, or something more complex—to every entry in a large dataset. GPUs are designed for this kind of work, enabling us to process millions of elements at once. Each GPU thread can handle one (or more) elements on its own, so there's no need for coordination. This makes elementwise computation highly efficient and naturally scalable. These operations are used in a bunch of different fields, like image processing, scientific simulation, machine learning, and financial modeling. Mastering this pattern gives us the ability to speed up not only basic arithmetic but also complex, specific tasks, and we can do all of this in the same elegant way. Once we get the hang of elementwise operations, a lot of complex algorithms start to look like simple variations on a theme.

The CuPy offers us a familiar, NumPy-like interface for elementwise operations—plus GPU acceleration under the hood. In most cases, switching from CPU to GPU only means changing our imports and array creation routines. The same broadcasting rules and syntax we already know from NumPy work seamlessly in CuPy, giving us instant access to the power of thousands of CUDA cores for every operation.

We will try to learn it with the following hands-on example:

Large-Scale Elementwise Arithmetic

Here, first, we will create two large arrays in GPU memory:

```
import cupy as cp
# Create two large arrays (ten million elements)
size = 10_000_000
a = cp.random.rand(size).astype(cp.float32)
b = cp.random.rand(size).astype(cp.float32)
```

We then perform elementwise arithmetic:

```
# Elementwise addition
sum_result = a + b
# Elementwise subtraction
diff_result = a - b
```

```
# Elementwise multiplication
prod_result = a * b
# Elementwise division (with epsilon for stability)
epsilon = 1e-8
div_result = a / (b + epsilon)
```

All these operations happen on the GPU, and every thread works independently. This is why the computation completes dramatically faster than if we used NumPy on large arrays—especially as data size grows.

Benefit of Broadcasting

One of the most powerful features of both NumPy and CuPy is broadcasting. Broadcasting lets us perform elementwise operations between arrays of different shapes, as long as their dimensions are compatible. For example, we can add a one-dimensional array to every row of a two-dimensional array:

```
# Broadcasting: add a (size,) array to each row of a (size,
100) array
array_2d = cp.random.rand(size, 100).astype(cp.float32)
broadcasted_result = array_2d + a[:, None]
```

The CuPy handles all of this on the GPU, mirroring the convenience of NumPy with massively improved speed.

So, to sum up, the key takeaways are:

- First, the elementwise operations are a core building block for parallel programming, perfectly matched to GPU hardware.
- The CuPy lets us write GPU-accelerated code with nearly the same syntax and broadcasting capabilities as NumPy.
- We can also quickly verify correctness and performance by comparing CPU and GPU outputs.

With this pattern mastered, we are prepared for more advanced parallel patterns.

Parallel Reduction for Summation

Parallel Reduction Overview

We often have to take a lot of data and turn it into a single value. On a CPU, you can usually do this with a loop or a built-in function like **sum()**. With a GPU, we want to use the parallel architecture to speed up this process. But if you're not careful, launching a kernel with every thread trying to add to a single total can quickly lead to bottlenecks and synchronization problems.

This is where parallel reduction comes in. It does this by having threads work together to add up elements in stages. This way, the problem gets smaller and smaller each step until there's just one value left. This approach reduces contention and makes the most of shared memory, which is a fast memory region on the GPU.

Building Parallel Reduction Kernel

To do this, we'll use a parallel sum reduction kernel with PyCUDA. This version uses a block-based approach, where each block sums its own part of the array using shared memory. Then, we finish the reduction on the CPU or with extra kernel launches if needed.

Setting up Data

First, we prepare our array on the host and transfer it to the GPU:

```
import numpy as np
import pycuda.autoinit
import pycuda.driver as drv
import pycuda.gpuarray as gpuarray
from pycuda.compiler import SourceModule
size = 1_048_576  # 1M elements for scalability demonstration
host_array = np.random.rand(size).astype(np.float32)
device_array = gpuarray.to_gpu(host_array)
```

Writing Reduction Kernel

Following is a block-level sum reduction kernel in CUDA C. In the below, we can see that each block computes a partial sum, stored in shared memory, and outputs one value per block:

```
kernel_code = """
extern "C"
__global__ void reduce_sum(float *g_idata, float *g_odata, int
n)
{
```

```
    extern __shared__ float sdata[];
    unsigned int tid = threadIdx.x;
    unsigned int i = blockIdx.x * blockDim.x * 2 +
threadIdx.x;
    float sum = 0;
    // Unrolling - read two elements per thread (if in range)
    if (i < n)
        sum += g_idata[i];
    if (i + blockDim.x < n)
        sum += g_idata[i + blockDim.x];
    sdata[tid] = sum;
    __syncthreads();
    // Reduce in shared memory
    for (unsigned int s = blockDim.x / 2; s > 0; s >>= 1) {
        if (tid < s)
            sdata[tid] += sdata[tid + s];
        __syncthreads();
    }
    // Write block result to global memory
    if (tid == 0)
        g_odata[blockIdx.x] = sdata[0];
}
"""
mod = SourceModule(kernel_code)
reduce_sum = mod.get_function("reduce_sum")
```

Configuring Launch Parameters

We then set up the block and grid sizes. We can use the shared memory for each block's sum:

```
threads_per_block = 512
```

```
B_gpu = gpuarray.to_gpu(B_host)
C_gpu = gpuarray.zeros((N, N), dtype=np.float32)
```

CUDA Kernel with Shared Memory Tiling

The following is a kernel for tiled matrix multiplication. Each thread block computes one TILE_SIZE x TILE_SIZE submatrix (tile) of the output.

```
kernel_code = f"""
#define TILE_SIZE {TILE_SIZE}
__global__ void matmul_tiled(float *A, float *B, float *C, int
N)
{{
    __shared__ float sA[TILE_SIZE][TILE_SIZE];
    __shared__ float sB[TILE_SIZE][TILE_SIZE];
    int row = blockIdx.y * TILE_SIZE + threadIdx.y;
    int col = blockIdx.x * TILE_SIZE + threadIdx.x;
    float sum = 0.0f;
    for (int t = 0; t < N / TILE_SIZE; ++t) {{
        // Collaborative loading into shared memory
        sA[threadIdx.y][threadIdx.x] = A[row * N + t *
TILE_SIZE + threadIdx.x];
        sB[threadIdx.y][threadIdx.x] = B[(t * TILE_SIZE +
threadIdx.y) * N + col];
        __syncthreads();
        // Compute partial sum
        for (int k = 0; k < TILE_SIZE; ++k) {{
            sum += sA[threadIdx.y][k] * sB[k][threadIdx.x];
        }}
        __syncthreads(); // Synchronize before loading new
tiles
    }}
    C[row * N + col] = sum;
```

```
}}
"""
mod = SourceModule(kernel_code)
matmul_tiled = mod.get_function("matmul_tiled")
```

Launching Kernel

Next, we then set up the grid and block configuration so each TILE_SIZE × TILE_SIZE tile is handled by a block.

```
block = (TILE_SIZE, TILE_SIZE, 1)
grid = (N // TILE_SIZE, N // TILE_SIZE, 1)
```

After this, we launch the kernel:

```
matmul_tiled(
    A_gpu, B_gpu, C_gpu, np.int32(N),
    block=block,
    grid=grid
)
```

Verification

We then finally bring the result back to the host and compare with NumPy's CPU multiplication for validation:

```
C_host = C_gpu.get()
C_ref = np.dot(A_host, B_host)
print("Are results close?", np.allclose(C_host, C_ref,
atol=1e-3))
```

When each block loads, it gets a tile of matrix A and a tile of matrix B from global memory into shared memory. Then, each thread in the block can use the loaded data multiple times without having to fetch it from global memory again. Instead of each thread reading a matrix row or column repeatedly from global memory, the threads fetch each needed element just once per tile. This significantly reduces the number of slow memory accesses and makes sure most accesses are to the fast, on-chip shared memory.

Parallel Map Pattern in Python

While elementwise arithmetic is powerful, many real applications require more involved transformations: non-linear functions, custom lookups, conditional logic, or even chaining multiple steps. The Python's built-in **`map()`** function, or comprehensions like **`[f(x) for x in xs]`**, offer a clean, expressive way to apply a function to each element of a collection. However, these patterns run sequentially and don't leverage the parallel capabilities of modern GPUs. As data grows, the performance limitations of sequential execution become pronounced, especially for large arrays or computationally expensive functions.

Parallel Map Pattern

The parallel map pattern provides a general solution: apply a user-defined function to each element of a dataset, in parallel, across many GPU threads. Each thread receives its own input value, computes the result, and writes it to the output array. This mirrors Python's **`map()`** but at the scale and speed of the GPU, providing an enormous performance boost for suitable workloads.

The strength of the parallel map pattern is its flexibility. We can use it for simple mathematical transforms, data normalization, or any operation that doesn't require interaction between elements. It also makes GPU programming more "Pythonic," letting us bring the expressive functional programming style to high-performance computing.

Mapping Map Pattern onto GPU Kernels

We will step through a hands-on demonstration. We'll use PyCUDA to apply a custom function to every element of an array—much like Python's **`map()`** but fully parallel.

Defining Custom Function

Let us consider that we want to apply the sigmoid function, common in machine learning:

```
def sigmoid(x):
    return 1.0 / (1.0 + np.exp(-x))
```

Now here, instead of looping in Python, we'll write a CUDA kernel that applies this to every element.

Preparing Data

Next, we generate a large input array:

```
import numpy as np
import pycuda.autoinit
```

```
import pycuda.driver as drv
import pycuda.gpuarray as gpuarray
from pycuda.compiler import SourceModule
N = 10_000_000
input_host = np.random.randn(N).astype(np.float32)
input_gpu = gpuarray.to_gpu(input_host)
output_gpu = gpuarray.empty_like(input_gpu)
```

Writing Parallel Map Kernel

Our kernel receives an input array, an output array, and the number of elements. Each thread processes one element independently:

```
kernel_code = """
__global__ void parallel_map(const float *input, float
*output, int n)
{
    int idx = blockIdx.x * blockDim.x + threadIdx.x;
    if (idx < n)
    {
        float x = input[idx];
        // Apply sigmoid function
        output[idx] = 1.0f / (1.0f + expf(-x));
    }
}
"""
mod = SourceModule(kernel_code)
parallel_map = mod.get_function("parallel_map")
```

Launching Kernel

We now proceed to configure the threads and blocks:

```
threads_per_block = 256
```

```
blocks_per_grid = (N + threads_per_block - 1) //
threads_per_block

parallel_map(
    input_gpu, output_gpu, np.int32(N),
    block=(threads_per_block, 1, 1),
    grid=(blocks_per_grid, 1)
)
```

Results Back to Host

After the computation completes, we then copy the results for verification:

```
output_host = output_gpu.get()
```

To confirm correctness, we then compare with the NumPy version:

```
sigmoid_np = 1.0 / (1.0 + np.exp(-input_host))

print("Outputs close?", np.allclose(output_host, sigmoid_np,
atol=1e-6))
```

This pattern is easy to extend to multiple inputs, more complex expressions, or even function parameters. We can implement ReLU, tanh, thresholding, or any mathematical function in the kernel body, then launch it for millions of elements in parallel. With this structure, even "complicated" functional operations become a matter of specifying the transformation, not worrying about performance or explicit loops.

Basic Histogram Computation

You'll find histograms are essential tools in data science, image processing, and many other scientific applications. They help us understand how data is distributed, analyze pixel intensities in images, or track frequencies in datasets. For small arrays, standard NumPy or CPU-based methods are usually fast enough for computing a histogram. But when you're dealing with data that's millions or billions of elements, or when you need real-time performance (like for streaming video or big-scale analytics), CPUs can have a hard time keeping up. These GPUs are great at doing lots of things at once, so they're perfect for speeding up histogram calculations, as long as we can deal with the challenges of making updates in parallel.

Computing GPU Histogram using CuPy

We will walk through a practical implementation using CuPy's RawKernel capabilities.

Preparing Data

Let's say we have a similar like before, a bunch of integer values (like pixel intensities):

```
import cupy as cp
import numpy as np
size = 10_000_000
nbins = 256  # For example, grayscale pixel values
data = cp.random.randint(0, nbins, size, dtype=cp.int32)
histogram = cp.zeros(nbins, dtype=cp.int32)
```

Writing Histogram Kernel

Basically, each thread handles part of the data and updates the relevant histogram bin using atomic operations. The shared memory holds each block's partial histogram, which minimizes global memory contention.

```
kernel_code = f"""
extern "C" __global__
void histogram(const int *data, int *hist, int N, int nbins)
{{
    extern __shared__ int s_hist[];
    int tid = threadIdx.x;
    int gid = blockIdx.x * blockDim.x + threadIdx.x;
    // Initialize shared histogram
    for (int i = tid; i < nbins; i += blockDim.x)
        s_hist[i] = 0;
    __syncthreads();
    // Accumulate in shared memory
    if (gid < N) {{
        int bin = data[gid];
        if (bin >= 0 && bin < nbins)
```

```
            atomicAdd(&s_hist[bin], 1);
    }}
    __syncthreads();
    // Merge shared histogram into global memory
    for (int i = tid; i < nbins; i += blockDim.x)
        atomicAdd(&hist[i], s_hist[i]);
}}
"""
module = cp.RawModule(code=kernel_code)
hist_kernel = module.get_function("histogram")
```

Configuring and Launching Kernel

We then set up the threads, blocks, and shared memory size:

```
threads_per_block = 256
blocks_per_grid = (size + threads_per_block - 1) //
threads_per_block
shared_mem_size = nbins * 4  # int32
hist_kernel(
    (blocks_per_grid,), (threads_per_block,),
    (data, histogram, size, nbins),
    shared_mem=shared_mem_size
)
```

Retrieve and Verify Results

We then copy the histogram back to the host and compare with the reference NumPy result:

```
hist_cpu = np.histogram(cp.asnumpy(data), bins=nbins,
range=(0, nbins))[0]
hist_gpu = histogram.get()
print("Are GPU and CPU histograms equal?",
np.array_equal(hist_cpu, hist_gpu))
```

From the above, we can see that each block merges its shared histogram into global memory, also using atomic adds. This approach delivers scalability and accuracy even for massive arrays and many bins.

To summarize, the histogram computation is a prime example of a data-intensive task that benefits from GPU acceleration, but only with careful use of shared memory and atomic operations. CuPy gives us the power to implement this classic parallel pattern efficie(ntly, so we can analyze large datasets, images, or streams at speed and scale.

Summary

To sum it up, we got better at designing and implementing common parallel patterns using GPU programming. We started by using elementwise operations on large arrays, learning to take advantage of CuPy's broadcasting and the NumPy-like syntax to do high-throughput computations on the GPU. We took it a step further and explored the parallel reduction pattern, using an efficient sum reduction kernel with PyCUDA. We learned how careful synchronization and shared memory usage enable large-scale data aggregation with minimal bottlenecks, and how this approach can be scaled for a wide range of reduction tasks.

We kept going with tiled matrix multiplication, talking about CUDA's shared memory and showing how tiling strategies really cut down on global memory traffic and boosted throughput for matrix computations. The parallel map pattern showed us how to generalize functional programming concepts—like Python's map—into highly parallel, custom GPU kernels for complex, elementwise operations. Finally, we took on histogram computation, where we combined shared memory and atomic operations to safely and efficiently handle concurrent updates, even when millions of threads target the same memory bins.

CHAPTER 5: INTRODUCTION TO KERNEL OPTIMIZATION

Choosing Block and Grid Sizes

As we develop more advanced GPU kernels, we begin to see that selecting the right thread block and grid sizes is one of the most important choices we can make for performance. While CUDA's massive parallelism enables us to process huge datasets quickly, hardware constraints—such as shared memory per block, register usage, and the total number of threads that can run on a multiprocessor at once—mean that not every block/grid configuration delivers optimal throughput. Poor choices can leave GPU resources underutilized, create memory bottlenecks, or even produce kernel launches that fail due to exceeding hardware limits.

The best-performing kernels strike a careful balance: large enough blocks to keep all SMs fully occupied, but not so large that they exhaust resources. The goal is to maximize **occupancy**—the proportion of available GPU resources that are actually being used for computation at any moment.

To quickly take you up to speed, the CUDA organizes threads into a hierarchy:

- One is the **Thread block** which is a group of threads that can cooperate via shared memory and synchronization (**`__syncthreads()`**). All threads in a block run on the same SM.
- And the other is the **Grid** which is the full set of all blocks launched by the kernel, spanning the entire dataset.

The choice of how many threads per block (also known as block size) and how many blocks per grid (also called grid size) affects how the work is partitioned and mapped to hardware. The standard practice is to use block sizes that are multiples of 32 (the warp size). Typical values are 128, 256, or 512 threads per block. But the ideal value depends on how the kernel uses registers, how much shared memory there is, and the size of the dataset.

Determining Optimal Configuration

The optimal block and grid size depends on three main factors:

- **Total problem size** (how many elements or tasks we want to process)
- **Hardware limits** (maximum threads per block, available shared memory, number of registers)
- **Kernel resource usage** (how much shared memory and how many registers each thread or block uses)

We can estimate a good starting point using the CUDA occupancy calculator provided by NVIDIA that models how many blocks can run simultaneously on each SM, given the kernel's resource usage.

Sample Program: Exploring Block and Grid Sizes

Let's say we want to launch a kernel to process a big 1D array.

```
import numpy as np
import cupy as cp
N = 10_000_000  # Total number of elements
a = cp.random.rand(N).astype(cp.float32)
b = cp.random.rand(N).astype(cp.float32)
c = cp.empty_like(a)
```

And assume that we want to compute **c[i] = a[i] + b[i]** using a custom kernel. We need to choose block and grid dimensions.

Picking Block Size and Launching Kernel

So here, we start with a block size of 256 or 512 (both multiples of the warp size). However, we hacve to make sure that it does not exceed the maximum allowed on our GPU (often 1024 threads/block).

```
threads_per_block = 256
blocks_per_grid = (N + threads_per_block - 1) //
threads_per_block
kernel_code = """
extern "C" __global__
void vector_add(const float* a, const float* b, float* c, int
n) {
    int idx = blockDim.x * blockIdx.x + threadIdx.x;
    if (idx < n) {
        c[idx] = a[idx] + b[idx];
    }
}
"""
mod = cp.RawModule(code=kernel_code)
vector_add = mod.get_function("vector_add")
vector_add(
    (blocks_per_grid,), (threads_per_block,),
```

```
    (a, b, c, N)
)
```

Evaluating Occupancy

The NVIDIA provides a web-based *Occupancy Calculator* (also available as an Excel sheet). To use it, we need to know:

- The block size (number of threads per block)
- The amount of shared memory used per block
- The number of registers used per thread (often reported by the CUDA compiler with **nvcc --ptxas-options=-v**)

For most basic kernels with minimal shared memory/register use, occupancy will be high even for large block sizes. If the kernel uses more shared memory or registers, occupancy may drop as these resources become bottlenecks.

Experimenting Performance

We can measure kernel execution time for various block sizes to see how throughput changes:

```
import time
for block_size in [64, 128, 256, 512, 1024]:
    grid_size = (N + block_size - 1) // block_size
    c_test = cp.empty_like(a)
    start = time.time()
    vector_add(
        (grid_size,), (block_size,),
        (a, b, c_test, N)
    )
    cp.cuda.Stream.null.synchronize()
    end = time.time()
    print(f"Block size {block_size}, Time: {end - start:.5f}
seconds")
```

We will observe that the fastest time often occurs with block sizes between 128 and 512, but this can vary based on our hardware and the kernel's complexity.

By picking thread block and grid sizes that work well together, we make sure our GPU kernels use the available hardware resources as well as possible. We combine hands-on experiments with tools like the occupancy calculator to find configurations that maximize throughput and achieve efficient, scalable parallel execution. This is a key part of how to optimize kernel performance.

Shared Memory for Data Reuse

Principle of Buffering

We've found that when we work with GPU programming, global memory transactions often become the bottleneck for throughput. Whenever a thread gets data from global memory, it has to pay a penalty for the delay. This delay can be much more than the time it takes to actually do the computation. If multiple threads within the same block need to access the same dataset, such as when neighboring threads work with overlapping data, or when a block processes a tile of a matrix or image, those repeated global memory fetches can add up quickly. One solution is CUDA's shared memory, which provides a small, user-managed, fast memory area local to each thread block. If we load data from global memory into shared memory just the once and then let all the threads in the block access that shared copy, we'll reduce memory traffic and boost our kernel's throughput.

That's where buffering comes in. It's basically a way to save some of the global memory so that different threads can use it over and over again without having to go back to the global memory each time. This approach works best when the data will be used more than once by different threads in a block, like in stencil computations, matrix tiling, or convolution operations.

1D Stencil Computation with Shared Memory

Let's take a look at how shared memory buffering is done in a typical GPU pattern, like a 1D stencil. In a stencil operation, each output element depends on its own value and its neighbors' values in an array. If each thread fetched its own neighbors from global memory, a lot of reads would be duplicated. When you use shared memory, each block works together to load a region that covers all the threads' needs, including neighbors.

Before we begin with, we first prepare the data to work upon:

```
import numpy as np
import pycuda.autoinit
import pycuda.driver as drv
import pycuda.gpuarray as gpuarray
from pycuda.compiler import SourceModule
```

```
N = 1024 * 1024
radius = 3  # How many neighbors to the left and right
input_host = np.random.rand(N).astype(np.float32)
output_host = np.zeros_like(input_host)
input_gpu = gpuarray.to_gpu(input_host)
output_gpu = gpuarray.empty_like(input_gpu)
```

Writing Shared Memory Kernel

Given below is a kernel where each block loads its segment, plus "halo" regions for neighbors, into shared memory. Later, each thread then computes its output using shared memory, reducing redundant global memory access.

```
kernel_code = f"""
#define RADIUS {radius}
#define BLOCK_SIZE 256
__global__ void stencil_1d(const float *input, float *output,
int N)
{{
    __shared__ float smem[BLOCK_SIZE + 2 * RADIUS];
    int tid = threadIdx.x;
    int global_idx = blockIdx.x * BLOCK_SIZE + tid;
    int smem_idx = tid + RADIUS;
    // Load center data
    if (global_idx < N)
        smem[smem_idx] = input[global_idx];
    // Load left halo
    if (tid < RADIUS && global_idx >= RADIUS)
        smem[smem_idx - RADIUS] = input[global_idx - RADIUS];
    // Load right halo
    if (tid >= BLOCK_SIZE - RADIUS && (global_idx + RADIUS) <
N)
```

```
        smem[smem_idx + RADIUS] = input[global_idx + RADIUS];
    __syncthreads();
    // Compute output (excluding boundary)
    if (global_idx >= RADIUS && global_idx < N - RADIUS) {{
        float sum = 0.0f;
        for (int j = -RADIUS; j <= RADIUS; ++j)
            sum += smem[smem_idx + j];
        output[global_idx] = sum / (2 * RADIUS + 1);
    }}
}}
"""
mod = SourceModule(kernel_code.replace("BLOCK_SIZE", "256"))
stencil_1d = mod.get_function("stencil_1d")
```

Launching Kernel

We then set up the configuration and run:

```
block_size = 256
grid_size = (N + block_size - 1) // block_size
stencil_1d(
    input_gpu, output_gpu, np.int32(N),
    block=(block_size, 1, 1), grid=(grid_size, 1)
)
```

Verifying Output

Next, we then compare the result to a reference NumPy implementation:

```
for i in range(radius, N - radius):
    output_host[i] = np.mean(input_host[i - radius:i + radius
+ 1])
output_gpu_host = output_gpu.get()
print("Results match?",
```

```
    np.allclose(output_host[radius:N-radius],
output_gpu_host[radius:N-radius], atol=1e-6))
```

So, without shared memory, each element and all its neighbors would be read from global memory for each thread. This will just lead to a ton of extra memory traffic. With shared memory, every value is fetched only once per block and then reused by every thread that needs it. As the block size and reuse increase, the savings get really high, often turning a memory-bound kernel into a compute-bound one.

Reducing Global Memory Accesses

Improper Bandwidth Utilization

Now that our kernels are getting more sophisticated, we're starting to see that not all memory accesses are created equal. When multiple threads in a warp access global memory, the GPU hardware tries to combine (or coalesce) these requests into as few memory transactions as possible. If threads access data in a regular, aligned, and contiguous fashion, the hardware can fetch the needed data in one go, using the full available bandwidth. If the access patterns are all over the place, it's possible that each thread's request might start its own transaction. This is called uncoalesced access, and it can really slow down your kernel performance by using too much of the memory bandwidth. And, one of the most common and costly inefficiencies in GPU programming is when the bandwidth isn't used properly because of uncoalesced loads and stores. We want to get the most out of our hardware, so we want to make sure that threads in the same warp (usually 32 threads) access consecutive memory locations whenever possible.

The answer is pretty simple: we just need to combine all the loads and stores worldwide. When threads are grouped in a warp, it's like they're all working together. They all get to access memory elements one after the other, and the first thread in a warp is the one that's in charge of accessing the first element of a memory address that's lined up in blocks. This lets the memory controller bundle requests together, fetching an entire block in a single operation. The result is maximal throughput—one memory transaction per warp instead of one per thread. We make this happen by arranging our data structures and access patterns so that threads with consecutive thread indices access consecutive addresses.

Sample Program: Coalesced vs. Uncoalesced Access

We will understand the difference with a simple array copy, and see how we can adjust our access patterns for coalescing. Following are the steps:

Suppose we have a large 1D array and want to copy data from one array to another on the device.

```
import numpy as np
```

```
import pycuda.autoinit
import pycuda.driver as drv
import pycuda.gpuarray as gpuarray
from pycuda.compiler import SourceModule
N = 1024 * 1024
input_host = np.random.rand(N).astype(np.float32)
input_gpu = gpuarray.to_gpu(input_host)
output_gpu = gpuarray.empty_like(input_gpu)
```

Uncoalesced Access Kernel

Let's say we can access elements with a stride, so each thread can access memory far from its neighbors as shown below:

```
kernel_uncoalesced = """
__global__ void copy_uncoalesced(const float *input, float
*output, int N, int stride)
{
    int idx = blockIdx.x * blockDim.x + threadIdx.x;
    if (idx < N/stride)
        output[idx] = input[idx * stride];
}
"""
mod_uncoalesced = SourceModule(kernel_uncoalesced)
copy_uncoalesced =
mod_uncoalesced.get_function("copy_uncoalesced")
```

Coalesced Access Kernel

In this version, each thread copies a consecutive element—ensuring full coalescence:

```
kernel_coalesced = """
__global__ void copy_coalesced(const float *input, float
*output, int N)
{
```

```
    int idx = blockIdx.x * blockDim.x + threadIdx.x;
    if (idx < N)
        output[idx] = input[idx];
}
"""
mod_coalesced = SourceModule(kernel_coalesced)
copy_coalesced = mod_coalesced.get_function("copy_coalesced")
```

Measuring Performance

We will compare the two approaches with the same block and grid sizes:

```
block_size = 256
grid_size = (N + block_size - 1) // block_size
import time
# Uncoalesced access with stride
stride = 32
output_uncoalesced = gpuarray.empty_like(input_gpu)
start = time.time()
copy_uncoalesced(
    input_gpu, output_uncoalesced, np.int32(N),
np.int32(stride),
    block=(block_size, 1, 1), grid=(grid_size // stride, 1)
)
drv.Context.synchronize()
end = time.time()
print(f"Uncoalesced copy time: {end - start:.5f} seconds")
# Coalesced access
output_coalesced = gpuarray.empty_like(input_gpu)
start = time.time()
copy_coalesced(
    input_gpu, output_coalesced, np.int32(N),
```

```
    block=(block_size, 1, 1), grid=(grid_size, 1)
)
drv.Context.synchronize()
end = time.time()
print(f"Coalesced copy time:   {end - start:.5f} seconds")
```

We will observe that the coalesced version completes much faster—often several times faster—because the hardware efficiently combines memory requests.

Data Alignment and Structure

To ensure coalescing in more complex scenarios (such as 2D or 3D arrays, or structures of arrays), arrange data so that consecutive threads in a warp always access consecutive memory locations. Avoid-of-array (SoA) layout (each field is stored as a separate array) is usually better for coalescing than array-of-structures (AoS), where different fields are interleaved.

So, we've got these kernels with coalesced access, our data all lined up, and thread access patterns that are pretty regular. That's how we get the full bandwidth of global memory working for us. This simple change turns underperforming kernels into highly efficient routines, letting our GPU applications scale smoothly as data size and computational demands grow.

Measuring Occupancy with CuPy Profiler

While we're working on optimizing our GPU kernels, our main goal is to keep the hardware as busy as possible. We want to saturate all the SMs with active threads and make full use of registers and memory resources. Occupancy shows how many threads are actually running compared to the maximum possible. High occupancy often, but not always, means high performance. If the occupancy is too low, a lot of GPU resources are just sitting there, unused. But if it's set too high, we might run out of registers or shared memory, which can lead to spills and slowdowns. It's key to understand and adjust occupancy if you want to write fast, efficient kernels.

CuPy Profiler Overview

The CuPy offers a convenient profiling API to help us understand what's happening when our kernels run. With the CuPy Profiler, we can collect kernel execution statistics—including occupancy metrics, registers per thread, memory usage, active warps, and more—directly from our Python environment. This makes it much easier to identify bottlenecks and iterate toward better performance, all without leaving our familiar workflow.

Collecting Kernel Statistics

The CuPy's **cupyx.profiler** module provides context managers for both function-level profiling and kernel-level statistics. We will use CuPy to launch a simple kernel and analyze its occupancy.

Following is an example of measuring occupancy for a vector addition operation:

```
import cupy as cp
from cupyx.profiler import benchmark
size = 10_000_000
a = cp.random.rand(size, dtype=cp.float32)
b = cp.random.rand(size, dtype=cp.float32)
def vector_add():
    cp.add(a, b, out=a)
# Profile the vector_add function
result = benchmark(vector_add, n_repeat=10)
print(result)
```

The **benchmark** function runs the operation several times, timing and profiling each run. Output includes timing, throughput, and can be configured to output kernel statistics if profiling tools are available.

For advanced metrics, we can use CuPy's raw kernel and set up kernel profiling using the CUDA Profiler API:

```
from cupyx.profiler import time_range
with time_range('Vector Add Profile', color_id=0):
    cp.add(a, b, out=a)
```

When running under Nsight Systems or Nsight Compute, this marks a time range and enables collection of per-kernel statistics.

Parsing and Interpreting Kernel Metrics

When profiling is enabled, the output includes details such as:

- **Active Warps per Multiprocessor** which indicates how many groups of 32 threads are running concurrently. Higher is generally better, up to hardware limits.
- **Registers per Thread** as it shows register pressure. Too many registers per thread may limit occupancy, as the total available is fixed per SM.

- **Shared Memory per Block** to reveal how much shared memory each block consumes. If blocks use too much, fewer can run at once, reducing occupancy.
- And, finally the **Occupancy** which is usually reported as a percentage or a ratio (e.g., 0.75), showing the fraction of theoretical maximum parallelism achieved.

Following is an example of Nsight Compute output for a kernel which might look like as shown below:

```
Grid Size: 39063 x 1 x 1

Block Size: 256 x 1 x 1

Registers per Thread: 32

Shared Memory per Block: 2.0 KB

Active Warps per SM: 24

Occupancy: 75%
```

If we observe these metrics very closely, we can be in a better position to answer questions such as:

- Are we using too many registers, limiting block concurrency?
- Does high shared memory per block reduce the number of active blocks?
- Are there too few active warps, leading to low throughput?

At any point, if you find that the occupancy is low due to registers, then try optimizing the kernel to use fewer variables or enable compiler flags to minimize register use. Similarly, if the shared memory limits occupancy, then try to reduce the shared memory usage per block or process smaller tiles.

Summary

In this chapter, we mainly looked at the practical side of kernel optimization and how to get the most out of GPU hardware. We started by looking at how thread block and grid sizes interact, and how that affects occupancy, parallel throughput, and hardware resource utilization. We learned to pick block and grid configurations that balance workload, memory usage, and computational capacity by doing hands-on experiments and using NVIDIA's occupancy calculator. Then, we checked out the power of shared memory by using buffering techniques.

Next, we kept going by checking out global memory access patterns, and we found out that misaligned and irregular accesses can really underutilize the available bandwidth. Finally, we used CuPy's profiling tools to collect live kernel statistics and get insights into occupancy, register and shared memory usage, and the number of active warps per multiprocessor. All of these things we've learned help us write efficient, resource-aware GPU programs that take full advantage of modern CUDA hardware.

Chapter 6: Working with PyCUDA and CuPy Features

Dynamic Kernel Compilation in PyCUDA

So far, we've been defining kernels as static code blocks in our Python scripts. We handwrite the CUDA C code as strings, compile it once, and launch them when needed. This works well for stable, fixed kernels. However, as our projects grow, we often find that flexibility, code generation, and parameter tuning are just as important as raw speed.

Dynamic Compilation Overview

Let's say we want to try out different kernel variations without having to re-write or manually recompile every time. Or maybe we want to generate kernels tailored to runtime parameters (like block sizes, unrolling factors, data types, or algorithmic tweaks), all from within the comfort of our Python session. This is where dynamic kernel compilation with PyCUDA really shines. It lets us generate, modify, and compile kernels on the fly, all while working seamlessly with our existing workflow.

The dynamic kernel compilation becomes valuable in several situations:

- When we want to adjust compile-time parameters (e.g., block size, data type, mathematical constants) based on runtime input.
- If we are building frameworks or tools that need to support many algorithmic variants without writing a new kernel for each case.
- For rapid prototyping, testing, or benchmarking, where fast turnaround and automation are essential.
- When hardware details or user preferences dictate different kernel implementations or optimizations.

With PyCUDA, we do not need to leave Python or manage temporary CUDA files. The kernel code is built as a Python string, parameterized, and compiled at runtime.

Parameterized Kernel for Vector Scaling

We will walk through a practical, incremental example using our existing PyCUDA setup. Assume our environment, driver, and dependencies are already configured, as established in earlier chapters. Suppose we want to multiply each element in a large array by a scaling factor. We want the flexibility to tune a compile-time unroll factor and also set the scaling constant at runtime—without hardcoding values or rewriting kernels.

Preliminary Data Config

Our workflow remains the same:

```
import numpy as np
import pycuda.autoinit
```

```
import pycuda.driver as drv
import pycuda.gpuarray as gpuarray
from pycuda.compiler import SourceModule
N = 2_000_000
host_array = np.random.rand(N).astype(np.float32)
device_array = gpuarray.to_gpu(host_array)
```

Building Parameterized Kernel

Suppose we want to try different loop unroll factors for performance. We generate the kernel code string, filling in the parameter dynamically:

```
def generate_scaling_kernel(unroll):
    return f"""
    __global__ void scale_unroll(float *data, float scale, int
n)
    {{
        int idx = blockDim.x * blockIdx.x + threadIdx.x;
        #pragma unroll
        for (int i = 0; i < {unroll}; ++i) {{
            int offset = idx + i * gridDim.x * blockDim.x;
            if (offset < n)
                data[offset] *= scale;
        }}
    }}
    """
unroll_factor = 4
kernel_code = generate_scaling_kernel(unroll_factor)
mod = SourceModule(kernel_code)
scale_unroll = mod.get_function("scale_unroll")
```

Launching Dynamically Compiled Kernel

We then configure the launch parameters based on our environment:

```
threads_per_block = 256
blocks_per_grid = (N + threads_per_block * unroll_factor - 1)
// (threads_per_block * unroll_factor)
scale_unroll(
    device_array, np.float32(2.5), np.int32(N),
    block=(threads_per_block, 1, 1),
    grid=(blocks_per_grid, 1)
)
```

Verifying and Experimenting

After the kernel runs, we then copy the data back to the host for validation:

```
result_host = device_array.get()
expected = host_array * 2.5
print("Result matches expected?", np.allclose(result_host,
expected))
```

Let's say we want to test a different unroll factor or try a different math operation here. We can just regenerate the kernel string and recompile, so there's no code duplication and no need to leave Python. This whole approach keeps our codebase lean, lets us experiment fast, and makes sure our GPU programs can adapt to any scenario, user, or setting without manual compilation or hardcoding.

CuPy for Custom Operations

Custom Universal Functions and Raw Kernels

So far, we've been using CuPy's ufuncs for a bunch of fast, elementwise operations, just like we did in NumPy. CuPy's universal functions are optimized, and its vectorized routines are mapped directly onto GPU hardware. This allows operations like addition, multiplication, trigonometric, and exponential functions to be written with clean, familiar syntax. These ufuncs are key to high-performance, elementwise array computation.

However, real-world scientific, engineering, or data-driven problems often demand more than just these built-in arithmetic or math operations. There are times when our application needs a transformation that isn't provided out of the box, such as a piecewise function, a thresholded nonlinear transformation, or a combination of mathematical and logical steps. In NumPy, we might use **np.vectorize** or **np.frompyfunc** to wrap custom logic, but these approaches do not accelerate on the GPU and aren't natively supported by CuPy. Standard ufuncs, while powerful, can become a limiting factor for advanced workflows that need custom logic at GPU speed.

The CuPy allows us to define our own universal functions using its **ElementwiseKernel** and **RawKernel** interfaces. With these tools, we can write specialized elementwise kernels directly in CUDA C or with CuPy's flexible Python API, then call them in array expressions just like built-in ufuncs. This approach lets us break out of the limitations of standard ufuncs and accelerate our own logic, however complex, on the GPU.

We will walk through how to create a custom universal function in CuPy and then define a more complex elementwise operation using a raw kernel.

Defining Custom Elementwise Universal Function

Suppose we want a function that applies a "leaky ReLU" transformation, a popular nonlinearity in machine learning:

```
import cupy as cp
leaky_relu = cp.ElementwiseKernel(
    'float32 x, float32 slope',      # Input arguments
    'float32 y',                     # Output argument
    'y = x > 0 ? x : slope * x;',# Operation in C syntax
    'leaky_relu'                     # Name
)
# Use our custom ufunc on a GPU array
a = cp.linspace(-5, 5, 10_000, dtype=cp.float32)
slope = 0.1
b = leaky_relu(a, slope)
```

This kernel is now a first-class ufunc: it broadcasts, works with arbitrary shapes, and executes entirely on the GPU.

Writing RawKernel for Specialized Logic

Let's say we need something even more specialized, like a function that adjusts the scaling based on different value ranges:

```
# CUDA kernel as a string
raw_kernel_code = r'''
extern "C" __global__
void piecewise_scale(const float* x, float* y, int n)
{
    int idx = blockDim.x * blockIdx.x + threadIdx.x;
    if (idx < n) {
        float val = x[idx];
        if (val < 0)
            y[idx] = val * 0.5f;
        else if (val < 1)
            y[idx] = val * 2.0f;
        else
            y[idx] = val * 0.1f;
    }
}
'''
mod = cp.RawModule(code=raw_kernel_code)
piecewise_scale = mod.get_function('piecewise_scale')
a = cp.linspace(-2, 3, 100_000, dtype=cp.float32)
b = cp.empty_like(a)
threads_per_block = 256
blocks_per_grid = (a.size + threads_per_block - 1) //
threads_per_block
piecewise_scale(
    (blocks_per_grid,), (threads_per_block,),
    (a, b, a.size)
)
```

Custom Kernels into Array Expressions

Once defined, these kernels fit smoothly into our workflow, working just like built-in ufuncs. We can use them in larger expressions, pass them as steps in a processing pipeline, or compose them with other array operations. For **ElementwiseKernel** functions, we even get broadcasting and mixed-type support, enabling easy integration into existing GPU workflows. And for **RawKernel** operations, we use standard CUDA launch syntax and coordinate data movement and memory management using CuPy arrays, keeping everything efficient and tightly integrated with the rest of our array processing code.

With these tools, we can confidently design, optimize, and scale custom GPU logic to match the complexity of any scientific or engineering problem.

Array Broadcasting and Indexing

CuPy's Broadcasting Rules

Broadcasting is one of the most powerful and convenient features in both NumPy and CuPy. It allows us to perform arithmetic or logical operations on arrays of different shapes, as long as they follow compatible broadcasting rules. This means we do not need to manually reshape, tile, or loop through arrays—CuPy automatically stretches smaller arrays across larger ones in memory-efficient ways, matching shapes as needed for the operation.

Broadcasting works by comparing the shapes of two (or more) arrays elementwise, starting from the trailing dimensions. If dimensions are equal, or if one of them is 1, the operation is permitted. CuPy then implicitly expands the size-1 dimension to match the larger dimension during computation, without actually copying or repeating any data in memory. These broadcasting rules let us write high-level mathematical and data manipulation code that is concise, expressive, and massively parallel. The result is GPU-accelerated array processing for both simple and very complex workflows, without explicit looping or manual memory management.

Sample Program: Broadcasting with CuPy Arrays

We will see how broadcasting simplifies elementwise and more advanced operations.

Elementwise Arithmetic with Different Shapes

Suppose we have a 2D array and a 1D array. We want to add the 1D array to each row of the 2D array:

```
import cupy as cp

rows, cols = 512, 128
```

```
matrix = cp.random.rand(rows, cols).astype(cp.float32)
vector = cp.linspace(1, 2, cols, dtype=cp.float32)
# Broadcasting: vector shape (128,) is broadcast to (512, 128)
result = matrix + vector  # Each row of 'matrix' gets 'vector' added
```

No loops, no manual expansion—CuPy handles the broadcasting behind the scenes.

Broadcasting across Multidimensional Arrays

We will multiply a 3D tensor with a 1D array:

```
tensor = cp.random.rand(32, 64, 128).astype(cp.float32)
scaling_factors = cp.linspace(0.1, 1.0, 128, dtype=cp.float32)
# scaling_factors broadcasts to (32, 64, 128)
scaled_tensor = tensor * scaling_factors
```

In the above, each element along the last dimension of the tensor is scaled by the corresponding value in **`scaling_factors`**, for every row and slice.

Advanced Indexing

The broadcasting is even more powerful when combined with advanced indexing. CuPy supports a wide range of indexing operations for selecting, modifying, or analyzing multidimensional arrays:

- **Integer array indexing:** Select arbitrary elements using index arrays.
- **Boolean masking:** Select elements that meet conditions.
- **Slice objects:** Select entire rows, columns, or arbitrary subarrays.

Integer Indexing

Suppose we want to select specific elements from a large 2D GPU array:

```
data = cp.random.rand(1024, 1024)
row_indices = cp.array([10, 200, 400])
col_indices = cp.array([5, 100, 800])
selected_elements = data[row_indices, col_indices]  # Selects (10,5), (200,100), (400,800)
```

Boolean Masking

We can filter elements with boolean masks, just as in NumPy:

```
mask = matrix > 0.5
filtered = matrix[mask]  # Returns all elements greater than
0.5
```

Multidimensional Slicing

Slice out blocks or subarrays for further operations:

```
sub_matrix = matrix[100:200, 50:90]
```

Many real tasks require both broadcasting and indexing—such as normalizing along an axis, centering data, or selectively updating elements.

```
mean = matrix.mean(axis=0)
centered = matrix - mean  # Broadcasting subtracts the mean
from each column
# Set all negative values to zero
matrix[matrix < 0] = 0
```

All of this happens without explicit Python loops, keeping our code both readable and blazingly fast. With broadcasting and advanced indexing, CuPy empowers us to express complex data operations in a few lines, harnessing the GPU's parallelism for real-world scientific, engineering, and analytics tasks.

Data Exchange between PyCUDA and CuPy

Why Data Sharing?

We sometimes find that neither PyCUDA nor CuPy alone offers everything we need. PyCUDA gives us fine-grained control, dynamic kernel compilation, and direct access to raw CUDA features. CuPy, on the other hand, provides a NumPy-like, expressive API for fast, elementwise array operations and rich high-level utilities. Some workflows may start with PyCUDA for a custom kernel or memory allocation, then switch to CuPy for convenient slicing, broadcasting, or high-level math. Sometimes, an external library or legacy code is built on PyCUDA, but the rest of the project is in CuPy.

The sharing of data efficiently between PyCUDA and CuPy becomes critical for performance and ease of development. We want to avoid extra device-to-host or host-to-device copies and keep all data on the GPU, passing ownership or views seamlessly between the two libraries.

CuPy and PyCUDA Interoperability

Both PyCUDA and CuPy manage device memory via their own GPU array classes:

- **`pycuda.gpuarray.GPUArray`**
- **`cupy.ndarray`**

Under the hood, both are wrappers around CUDA device pointers and memory pools, but their Python interfaces are different. Luckily, they both expose ways to create one's array from the device pointer of the other, without extra copies.

Converting PyCUDA to CuPy ndarray

So, let's say we've got a PyCUDA GPUArray (like from a custom kernel):

```
import pycuda.gpuarray as gpuarray
import pycuda.autoinit
import numpy as np
import cupy as cp
arr_host = np.arange(10_000, dtype=np.float32)
arr_gpu_py = gpuarray.to_gpu(arr_host)
```

We can create a CuPy ndarray view of this memory directly:

```
ptr = arr_gpu_py.gpudata  # Raw device pointer
shape = arr_gpu_py.shape
dtype = arr_gpu_py.dtype
arr_cupy = cp.ndarray(shape, dtype=dtype,
memptr=cp.cuda.MemoryPointer(cp.cuda.UnownedMemory(
    int(ptr), arr_gpu_py.nbytes, arr_gpu_py), 0))
```

In the above, the **`cp.cuda.UnownedMemory`** wraps the PyCUDA memory without copying, and **`MemoryPointer`** tells CuPy to use it as its own array data. The original PyCUDA GPUArray object keeps the memory alive as long as either object exists.

Converting CuPy to PyCUDA GPUArray

Suppose we have processed data in CuPy:

```
arr_cupy = cp.arange(10_000, dtype=cp.float32)
```

We can create a PyCUDA GPUArray view:

```
import pycuda.driver as drv
import pycuda.gpuarray as gpuarray
ptr = arr_cupy.data.ptr
shape = arr_cupy.shape
dtype = np.dtype(str(arr_cupy.dtype))
gpudata = drv.DeviceAllocation(ptr)
arr_gpu_py = gpuarray.GPUArray(shape, dtype, gpudata)
```

The PyCUDA now manages the same device memory. Both objects refer to the same GPU buffer, and no data is copied.

We can efficiently bridge PyCUDA and CuPy by exchanging device pointers and using memory views. This avoids redundant device-host transfers and makes the most of both libraries. This technique makes it possible to have smooth, high-performance mixed-library workflows for advanced GPU projects.

Summary

To sum it up quickly, we came to an understanding of PyCUDA and CuPy, and we expanded our toolkit for both low-level and high-level GPU programming in Python. We checked out dynamic kernel compilation in PyCUDA, which gave us the power to generate and tune CUDA code at runtime right from our Python environment. We also learned to extend CuPy with custom elementwise kernels to get around the limitations of standard universal functions.

We then used broadcasting and advanced indexing in CuPy to perform complex, multidimensional array operations, all without using loops. We then got PyCUDA and CuPy working together by swapping device arrays using pointer-based conversions. This technique lets us mix custom kernels, low-level memory management, and high-level numerical workflows while avoiding unnecessary copies or host-device transfers. With these skills, we're all set to develop solid, flexible GPU applications that combine the strengths of both PyCUDA and CuPy for research, engineering, or production pipelines that need both control and flexibility.

CHAPTER 7: PRACTICAL SORTING AND SEARCH

GPU-Accelerated Bitonic Sort

Sorting is a cornerstone operation in data processing, analytics, and simulation workflows. As datasets continue to grow, efficient sorting becomes increasingly important. While the CPU provides robust and versatile sorting algorithms, not all of them map well to massively parallel architectures like GPUs.

Introduction to Bitonic Sort

Bitonic sort is a classic, comparison-based sorting algorithm designed for parallel hardware. Unlike quicksort or mergesort, which require adaptive branching and recursive division, bitonic sort follows a fixed sequence of compare-and-swap operations, organized into predefined stages. Every step can be mapped to a group of independent, regular GPU threads. This predictability makes bitonic sort particularly suitable for GPUs, enabling large batches of data to be sorted simultaneously with high throughput and minimal synchronization.

The GPU-accelerated bitonic sort offers compelling benefits:

- Every stage of the algorithm can run thousands of compare-and-swap operations concurrently.
- The regularity and lack of data-dependent branches result in efficient GPU kernels.
- Useful for applications where latency is critical or data must be sorted on the fly, such as simulation pipelines, graphics rendering, or real-time analytics.

The key idea is to iteratively build and merge bitonic sequences (arrays where elements first monotonically increase and then decrease, or vice versa) through a fixed set of compare-and-swap stages. Each stage involves a specific pattern of pairwise comparisons, which are well suited for parallel threads. The number of stages and the pairs compared at each step are determined solely by the size of the input. This means that the kernel logic can be precomputed and launched in a series of steps, with synchronization between each stage.

GPU Bitonic Sort in Action

We will put this theory into practice by building a simple, yet effective, bitonic sort for 1D arrays of float32 values using PyCUDA with following steps:

Before we begin with, we get the data prepared as usual:

```
import numpy as np
import pycuda.autoinit
import pycuda.driver as drv
import pycuda.gpuarray as gpuarray
from pycuda.compiler import SourceModule
```

```
import time
# For best performance, use a power-of-two array length
N = 2**15  # 32768 elements
arr_host = np.random.rand(N).astype(np.float32)
arr_gpu = gpuarray.to_gpu(arr_host)
```

Bitonic Sort Kernel

The following kernel implements a single stage of the bitonic sort. Each thread compares and conditionally swaps two elements, depending on the current stage and direction.

```
bitonic_kernel_code = """
__global__ void bitonic_step(float *data, int j, int k, int n)
{
    unsigned int idx = threadIdx.x + blockDim.x * blockIdx.x;
    if (idx >= n) return;
    unsigned int ixj = idx ^ j;
    if (ixj > idx) {
        if ((idx & k) == 0) {
            if (data[idx] > data[ixj]) {
                float tmp = data[idx];
                data[idx] = data[ixj];
                data[ixj] = tmp;
            }
        } else {
            if (data[idx] < data[ixj]) {
                float tmp = data[idx];
                data[idx] = data[ixj];
                data[ixj] = tmp;
            }
        }
```

```
    }
}
"""
```

```
mod = SourceModule(bitonic_kernel_code)
bitonic_step = mod.get_function("bitonic_step")
```

Host-Side Logic and Performance Measure

The Bitonic sort is organized into a double loop, with outer and inner stages. We repeatedly launch the kernel, specifying the current **j** and **k** values:

```
def gpu_bitonic_sort(arr_gpu, n, threads_per_block=256):
    blocks_per_grid = (n + threads_per_block - 1) //
threads_per_block
    for k in [2**i for i in range(1, int(np.log2(n)) + 1)]:
        for j in [2**i for i in range(int(np.log2(k)), -1, -
1)]:
            bitonic_step(
                arr_gpu, np.int32(j), np.int32(k),
np.int32(n),
                block=(threads_per_block, 1, 1),
grid=(blocks_per_grid, 1)
            )
start_gpu = time.time()
gpu_bitonic_sort(arr_gpu, N)
drv.Context.synchronize()
end_gpu = time.time()
sorted_gpu = arr_gpu.get()
arr_host_copy = arr_host.copy()
start_cpu = time.time()
arr_host_copy.sort()
end_cpu = time.time()
```

```
print("GPU bitonic sort time: {:.4f} sec".format(end_gpu - start_gpu))
print("CPU numpy sort time:   {:.4f} sec".format(end_cpu - start_cpu))
print("Are results close?", np.allclose(arr_host_copy, sorted_gpu, atol=1e-6))
```

Based on what we've seen, GPU-accelerated bitonic sort is a lot better than CPU-based sorts, especially for medium-sized and batch-processing scenarios. On large arrays with a power of two, we can expect the GPU version to be several times faster than the CPU, depending on the hardware and kernel tuning. The gap gets even bigger when you're dealing with multiple arrays or when it's part of a bigger GPU-based workflow, where the data stays on the device the whole time.

Radix Sort on Integer Arrays

We have already seen how bitonic sort works efficiently on the GPU due to its regular, comparison-based structure and fixed set of parallel steps. However, comparison-based algorithms like bitonic sort are not always the most efficient, especially when sorting large arrays of integers. Radix sort takes a fundamentally different approach by sorting based on the binary representation of the numbers, one group of bits at a time, which removes the need for comparisons altogether.

On the GPU, this means radix sort can work through the dataset in a series of fast, deterministic passes, distributing and gathering elements based on digit values, while exploiting parallelism at every step.

Running Radix Sort with CuPy

We will prepare a large integer array for our better understanding:

```
import cupy as cp
import numpy as np
import time
N = 2**20  # 1,048,576 integers
arr_host = np.random.randint(0, 10_000_000, size=N, dtype=np.int32)
arr_cupy = cp.array(arr_host)
```

The CuPy's **cp.sort** handles integer arrays using radix sort under the hood for large enough sizes as shown below:

```
start_gpu = time.time()
sorted_cupy = cp.sort(arr_cupy)
cp.cuda.Stream.null.synchronize()
end_gpu = time.time()
sorted_host_radix = cp.asnumpy(sorted_cupy)
```

Running Bitonic Sort with PyCUDA

We will now use the bitonic sort implementation we have developed previously. Since bitonic sort works on float data, convert the integer array to float for a fair technical comparison:

```
import pycuda.gpuarray as gpuarray
import pycuda.autoinit
arr_gpu_bitonic = gpuarray.to_gpu(arr_host.astype(np.float32))
start_bitonic = time.time()
gpu_bitonic_sort(arr_gpu_bitonic, N)  # This function was
defined in our last topic
pycuda.autoinit.context.synchronize()
end_bitonic = time.time()
sorted_host_bitonic = arr_gpu_bitonic.get()
```

Next, we will then print the timings and check result accuracy:

```
# Compare timing
print("CuPy radix sort time:   {:.4f} sec".format(end_gpu -
start_gpu))
print("PyCUDA bitonic sort time: {:.4f}
sec".format(end_bitonic - start_bitonic))
# Check if both sorting results match the CPU reference
reference = np.sort(arr_host)
match_radix = np.allclose(reference, sorted_host_radix)
```

```
match_bitonic = np.allclose(reference, sorted_host_bitonic,
atol=1)
print("Radix sort matches reference:", match_radix)
print("Bitonic sort matches reference:", match_bitonic)
```

The above Radix sort on the GPU, as implemented and exposed through CuPy's sort API, is a prime example of using digit-based parallel partitioning for high-speed integer sorting. In practical experiments, the radix sort clearly outpaces bitonic sort for large arrays, confirming its place as the go-to algorithm for high-throughput, GPU-based integer sorting tasks.

Parallel Linear Search Kernel

Why Parallel Linear Search?

It's a classic operation, fundamental to database queries, pattern matching, and data analytics. Usually, linear search is done sequentially. The CPU checks one element at a time, moving through the array until it finds the target. It's straightforward, but it's a bit of a slow process for large datasets because it only checks one element per CPU cycle.

The GPUs have thousands of threads, which makes them much faster for this task. If we assign each thread a part of the array (or even just one element), we can check a bunch of elements at the same time. The search is finished as soon as any thread finds the target. This model is great for big datasets where you don't know where the target is, and when you need to run a bunch of searches at once. It's not always the best choice for sorting arrays, as other methods like binary search or scan-based search can be faster. But for unsorted data or bulk pattern queries, it can speed things up significantly compared to the traditional CPU approach.

Writing Parallel Linear Search Kernel

We'll be developing a parallel linear search kernel to find a target integer in a large array. First, we prepare the data as usual:

```
import numpy as np
import pycuda.autoinit
import pycuda.driver as drv
import pycuda.gpuarray as gpuarray
from pycuda.compiler import SourceModule
N = 2_000_000
```

```
target_value = 123456
# Place the target at a random position
arr_host = np.random.randint(0, 1_000_000, N).astype(np.int32)
rand_index = np.random.randint(0, N)
arr_host[rand_index] = target_value  # Ensure target is
present
arr_gpu = gpuarray.to_gpu(arr_host)
```

Write Parallel Search Kernel

The kernel launches one thread per element, each comparing its value to the target. If found, it writes its index to an output array using atomic operations to avoid race conditions.

```
kernel_code = """
__global__ void parallel_search(const int *data, int
*found_idx, int target, int n)
{
    int idx = blockIdx.x * blockDim.x + threadIdx.x;
    if (idx < n && data[idx] == target) {
        atomicMin(found_idx, idx); // Record the lowest index
where found
    }
}
"""
mod = SourceModule(kernel_code)
parallel_search = mod.get_function("parallel_search")
```

Prepare Output Buffer

We then initialize a device-side buffer to store the result:

```
found_idx = gpuarray.to_gpu(np.array([N], dtype=np.int32))  #
Initialize with max value
```

Launch Kernel

After this, configure the block and grid sizes, then run the search:

```
threads_per_block = 256
blocks_per_grid = (N + threads_per_block - 1) //
threads_per_block
parallel_search(
    arr_gpu, found_idx, np.int32(target_value), np.int32(N),
    block=(threads_per_block, 1, 1), grid=(blocks_per_grid, 1)
)
drv.Context.synchronize()
result = found_idx.get()[0]
if result < N:
    print(f"Target found at index {result}")
else:
    print("Target not found")
```

Compare with Sequential Search

Finally, we will check the CPU performance for context:

```
import time
start_cpu = time.time()
for i, val in enumerate(arr_host):
    if val == target_value:
        cpu_idx = i
        break
end_cpu = time.time()
print(f"CPU search index: {cpu_idx}, time: {end_cpu -
start_cpu:.4f} sec")
```

For large arrays, the parallel kernel dramatically reduces search time, since all elements are checked in parallel. In practical settings, the overall latency is limited only by the slowest threads or the time taken to launch and synchronize the kernel, which is often orders of magnitude faster than sequential CPU search for big arrays.

This approach is highly scalable, and the same principle can be extended to search for multiple targets, count occurrences, or even run more complex match operations in parallel.

Merging Results on Host Side

Why Merge Results?

So far, we have learned to accelerate sorting and search tasks on the GPU using both PyCUDA and CuPy. Each kernel processes massive arrays in parallel and, in many cases, produces partial results or per-block outputs that must be collected, merged, or finalized on the host (CPU) to complete the workflow. Whether sorting large datasets in segments or running parallel search queries, merging results on the host is an essential pattern for correctness, scalability, and integration with downstream tasks.

Here are some typical situations where host-side merging comes in handy:

- If the array is divided into chunks and sorted in parallel, these sorted segments must be merged into one sorted array.
- If multiple positions or hits are found by different threads or blocks, the smallest (or all) matching indices must be collected and resolved on the CPU.
- When splitting data across GPU blocks or separate kernel launches, elements near chunk boundaries may require special attention during merging to maintain order and accuracy.

Collecting Device Results

When you run a GPU kernel for sorting or searching, first you transfer the result arrays from the device to the host using **`.get()`** in PyCUDA or **`cp.asnumpy()`** in CuPy:

```
# For sorting
sorted_gpu = arr_gpu.get()        # PyCUDA
sorted_cupy = cp.asnumpy(arr_cupy_sorted)  # CuPy
# For search (partial indices)
partial_indices_gpu = found_idx_gpu.get()
```

Merging Sorted Chunks

Let's say we sorted the array in segments. For large arrays or limited memory, we could use separate kernels for each segment. The host just needs to combine these sorted segments into a single sorted output.

```
import numpy as np
# Example: merging two sorted arrays
segment1 = np.sort(np.random.randint(0, 100, size=5000))
segment2 = np.sort(np.random.randint(0, 100, size=5000))
merged = np.empty(len(segment1) + len(segment2),
dtype=segment1.dtype)
i = j = k = 0
while i < len(segment1) and j < len(segment2):
    if segment1[i] < segment2[j]:
        merged[k] = segment1[i]
        i += 1
    else:
        merged[k] = segment2[j]
        j += 1
    k += 1
# Copy any remaining elements
merged[k:] = segment1[i:] if i < len(segment1) else
segment2[j:]
```

For more than two chunks, use **np.merge1d** or Python's **heapq.merge()** for general K-way merging.

Merging Search Results

How about if we did a parallel search, with each block or kernel writing its result index (or -1 if it didn't find anything) into an array? We collect all valid indices on the host and pick the smallest one (or all matches, if needed).

```
partial_indices = np.array([12, -1, -1, 78, -1])  # Example
output from GPU
hits = partial_indices[partial_indices != -1]
if len(hits) > 0:
    print("Target found at indices:", hits)
    print("First occurrence:", hits.min())
```

```
else:
    print("Target not found")
```

When merging results from different segments or partial searches, take care to:

- **Check for duplicates** at segment boundaries (e.g., overlapping elements included in multiple blocks).
- **Preserve overall order** when merging sorted chunks (no out-of-place elements).
- **Verify index correctness** for search—ensure global positions, not just within-chunk indices.

After merging, then try to compare the final result to a reference computed entirely on the CPU to ensure correctness:

```
reference_sorted = np.sort(complete_input_array)
if np.array_equal(merged, reference_sorted):
    print("Merged sort result is correct!")
else:
    print("Merged sort result is incorrect.")
# For search, confirm all positions contain the target
if all(complete_input_array[idx] == target_value for idx in
hits):
    print("Search indices are valid.")
else:
    print("One or more search indices are incorrect.")
```

So, we take the strengths of both approaches and combine them to create solid solutions for sorting, searching, and analyzing large amounts of data.

Summary

To sum it up, we took a look at how GPU acceleration changes things around with sorting and searching, and it turns out it's pretty darn impressive for handling large amounts of data. We started by understanding the structure and parallelism of bitonic sort, then implemented it with PyCUDA to show how GPUs can run thousands of compare-and-swap operations at the same time. By timing and validating bitonic sort against its CPU counterpart, we learned to appreciate its predictable, stage-based design for parallel hardware. Then, we used radix sort for integer arrays, taking advantage of CuPy's efficient, digit-based partitioning kernels. We did some performance comparisons, and it looks like radix sort, with its non-comparison, bucket-based logic, does a lot better than bitonic sort for large integer datasets.

Then, we shifted our focus to search. We designed and implemented a parallel linear search kernel that leveraged the GPU's thread-level parallelism. This showed the clear advantage of this approach over traditional sequential search for massive arrays. We finally put all these techniques together by combining device-side results on the host—like combining sorted segments or collecting search indices—and checked that our workflows were correct by comparing them to reference CPU solutions. By doing these hands-on exercises, we've figured out how to design GPU-accelerated sorting and search pipelines that are both fast and strong enough to handle real-world data challenges.

CHAPTER 8: LINEAR ALGEBRA ESSENTIALS ON GPU

Dense Vector and Matrix Operations with cuBLAS

Introduction to cuBLAS

The cuBLAS is NVIDIA's GPU-accelerated library designed to deliver highly optimized linear algebra operations—covering everything from simple vector additions to large-scale matrix-matrix multiplications. Its routines are written, tuned, and maintained by NVIDIA to get the absolute best out of CUDA-capable hardware, leveraging specialized instructions, memory layouts, and batched parallelism that would be challenging to reproduce by hand.

The cuBLAS follows the classic BLAS (Basic Linear Algebra Subprograms) API, familiar to users from the scientific and engineering world, but supercharges it for the GPU. This makes cuBLAS the go-to choice for dense linear algebra workloads in machine learning, simulation, signal processing, and beyond.

Although we can write custom CUDA kernels for matrix and vector operations (as we have practiced in earlier chapters), these hand-written kernels rarely match the efficiency and performance of cuBLAS routines. The reasons are:

- cuBLAS uses advanced techniques such as tiling, register blocking, memory coalescing, and fusion of operations.
- The library dynamically adapts to the GPU architecture and optimizes for hardware features.
- cuBLAS covers a wide range of routines, from the most basic (vector add) to advanced (LU decomposition), saving us from implementing and debugging these ourselves.

cuBLAS with CuPy

The CuPy offers a seamless Python interface to cuBLAS, so we can call high-performance GPU routines as easily as we call NumPy functions.

Dense Vector Operations

We will start with a simple vector addition and dot product.

```
import cupy as cp
import numpy as np
import time
N = 1_000_000
a = cp.random.rand(N, dtype=cp.float32)
```

```
b = cp.random.rand(N, dtype=cp.float32)
# Vector addition (elementwise sum)
start = time.time()
c = a + b  # Uses cuBLAS under the hood
cp.cuda.Stream.null.synchronize()
elapsed_add = time.time() - start
# Dot product (inner product)
start = time.time()
dot_result = cp.dot(a, b)  # cuBLAS-accelerated
cp.cuda.Stream.null.synchronize()
elapsed_dot = time.time() - start
print(f"Vector add (cuBLAS) time: {elapsed_add:.5f} sec")
print(f"Dot product (cuBLAS) time: {elapsed_dot:.5f} sec")
```

Dense Matrix-Matrix Multiplication

Matrix multiplication is the ultimate showcase for cuBLAS. We will compute a product of two dense matrices:

```
M, K, N_ = 2048, 2048, 2048
A = cp.random.rand(M, K, dtype=cp.float32)
B = cp.random.rand(K, N_, dtype=cp.float32)
start = time.time()
C = cp.matmul(A, B)  # cuBLAS-powered GEMM
cp.cuda.Stream.null.synchronize()
elapsed_mm = time.time() - start
print(f"Matrix multiply (cuBLAS) time: {elapsed_mm:.5f} sec")
```

Manual Kernel for Comparison

Suppose we try a simple, hand-written matrix multiplication kernel (without memory tiling or other cuBLAS optimizations):

```
from cupy import RawKernel
```

```
matmul_kernel = RawKernel(r'''
extern "C" __global__
void matmul(const float* A, const float* B, float* C, int M,
int K, int N) {
    int row = blockDim.y * blockIdx.y + threadIdx.y;
    int col = blockDim.x * blockIdx.x + threadIdx.x;
    if (row < M && col < N) {
        float sum = 0.0f;
        for (int i = 0; i < K; ++i)
            sum += A[row * K + i] * B[i * N + col];
        C[row * N + col] = sum;
    }
}
''', 'matmul')
C_manual = cp.zeros((M, N_), dtype=cp.float32)
block = (16, 16)
grid = (N_ // block[0], M // block[1])
start = time.time()
matmul_kernel(
    grid, block,
    (A, B, C_manual, np.int32(M), np.int32(K), np.int32(N_))
)
cp.cuda.Stream.null.synchronize()
elapsed_manual = time.time() - start
print(f"Matrix multiply (manual kernel) time:
{elapsed_manual:.5f} sec")
```

Performance Comparison and Validation

After timing both versions, validate their correctness and compare their speeds:

```
max_diff = cp.max(cp.abs(C - C_manual))
```

```
print("Maximum difference between cuBLAS and manual kernel:", max_diff)

print(f"Speedup (cuBLAS / manual): {elapsed_manual / elapsed_mm:.2f}x")
```

Typically, we will observe:

- cuBLAS is dramatically faster (often 5–10×) than a naive kernel.
- cuBLAS produces results with high numerical accuracy.
- As problem sizes scale, the efficiency gap widens, especially for large matrix products or batched operations.

The tight integration of CuPy makes it super easy to use these routines. It's like writing NumPy code, but way faster. This makes it possible to scale scientific, engineering, and machine learning workflows to modern GPUs with no problems at all.

Simple Matrix–Vector Multiplication

Matrix–vector multiplication is a fundamental linear algebra operation. It appears throughout scientific computing, data analysis, and machine learning, forming the backbone of neural network inference, iterative solvers, and more. Efficient implementation of this operation is crucial for scalable, high-performance pipelines on modern hardware.

So here in this topic, we will first handcraft a simple matrix–vector multiplication kernel in PyCUDA to build intuition and practice with kernel design. Next, we will use cuBLAS (via CuPy) to perform the same computation using highly optimized library routines. Finally, we will compare the correctness and performance of both approaches, demonstrating the value of leveraging cuBLAS for dense linear algebra on the GPU.

Matrix–Vector Multiplication with PyCUDA

Suppose we have a matrix AAA of size M×NM \times NM×N and a vector xxx of length NNN, and we want to compute the result y=A×xy = A \times xy=A×x. We will proceed with following steps:

- Preparing Data

```
import numpy as np

import pycuda.autoinit

import pycuda.driver as drv

import pycuda.gpuarray as gpuarray
```

```
from pycuda.compiler import SourceModule
import cupy as cp
import time
M, N = 2048, 2048
A_host = np.random.rand(M, N).astype(np.float32)
x_host = np.random.rand(N).astype(np.float32)
A_gpu = gpuarray.to_gpu(A_host)
x_gpu = gpuarray.to_gpu(x_host)
y_gpu = gpuarray.zeros(M, dtype=np.float32)
```

- PyCUDA Kernel Implementation

```
kernel_code = """
__global__ void matvec(const float *A, const float *x, float
*y, int M, int N)
{
    int row = blockIdx.x * blockDim.x + threadIdx.x;
    if (row < M) {
        float sum = 0.0f;
        for (int col = 0; col < N; ++col)
            sum += A[row * N + col] * x[col];
        y[row] = sum;
    }
}
"""
mod = SourceModule(kernel_code)
matvec = mod.get_function("matvec")
```

- Launch Kernel

```
threads_per_block = 256
```

```
blocks_per_grid = (M + threads_per_block - 1) //
threads_per_block
start = time.time()
matvec(
    A_gpu, x_gpu, y_gpu, np.int32(M), np.int32(N),
    block=(threads_per_block, 1, 1), grid=(blocks_per_grid, 1)
)
drv.Context.synchronize()
elapsed_pycuda = time.time() - start
y_result_pycuda = y_gpu.get()
```

Matrix–Vector Multiplication with cuBLAS

The CuPy provides a direct and highly optimized matrix–vector multiplication using the **cp.dot** function or **@** operator. This calls cuBLAS's **gemv** routine under the hood.

```
A_cupy = cp.array(A_host)
x_cupy = cp.array(x_host)
start = time.time()
y_cupy = cp.dot(A_cupy, x_cupy)
cp.cuda.Stream.null.synchronize()
elapsed_cublas = time.time() - start
y_result_cublas = cp.asnumpy(y_cupy)
```

We can also check that the two GPU results are nearly identical and measure the speedup:

```
max_diff = np.max(np.abs(y_result_pycuda - y_result_cublas))
print("Maximum difference:", max_diff)
print(f"PyCUDA kernel time: {elapsed_pycuda:.5f} sec")
print(f"cuBLAS (CuPy) time: {elapsed_cublas:.5f} sec")
print(f"Speedup (PyCUDA / cuBLAS): {elapsed_pycuda /
elapsed_cublas:.2f}x")
```

For real-world applications, relying on cuBLAS for dense matrix–vector (and matrix–matrix) operations is almost always preferred, unless our needs are extremely specialized or our data layout is non-standard. The speed, stability, and simplicity make it the foundation of scientific and ML computing on the GPU.

Batched GEMM for Multiple Matrices

Why Batched GEMM?

In many scientific, engineering, and machine learning applications, we often need to perform matrix multiplications not just on a single pair of matrices, but on many pairs—sometimes hundreds or thousands—at once. Examples include mini-batch neural network inference, 3D graphics transformations, and simulation of physical systems. Executing each multiplication one at a time in a loop (sequentially) does not fully utilize the GPU, leading to wasted cycles and underwhelming throughput.

The cuBLAS provides a batched GEMM (General Matrix–Matrix Multiplication) interface that allows us to submit a stack of matrix multiplication tasks at once. The library processes all batches in parallel, delivering huge gains in performance and total throughput compared to looping over single multiplications.

Executing Batched GEMM with cuBLAS

We will walk through performing batched matrix multiplications and comparing the performance to sequential execution.

Prepare Multiple Matrices

Suppose we want to multiply 1000 pairs of 32×3232 \times 3232×32 matrices:

```
import cupy as cp
import numpy as np
import time
batch_size = 1000
M = N = K = 32
A = cp.random.rand(batch_size, M, K).astype(cp.float32)
B = cp.random.rand(batch_size, K, N).astype(cp.float32)
```

Batched GEMM with CuPy

The CuPy leverages cuBLAS batched GEMM behind the scenes when we call **`cp.matmul`** or the **`@`** operator on arrays with matching batch dimensions.

```
start = time.time()
C_batched = cp.matmul(A, B)  # Shape: (batch_size, M, N)
cp.cuda.Stream.null.synchronize()
elapsed_batched = time.time() - start
```

Sequential Matrix Multiplication

We will compute the same result, but one pair at a time, to see how much throughput is lost:

```
C_sequential = cp.empty_like(C_batched)
start = time.time()
for i in range(batch_size):
    C_sequential[i] = cp.matmul(A[i], B[i])
cp.cuda.Stream.null.synchronize()
elapsed_sequential = time.time() - start
```

And then finally, confirm that both methods give the same answer and see how much faster batched GEMM is:

```
max_diff = cp.max(cp.abs(C_batched - C_sequential))
print("Maximum difference between batched and sequential:",
float(max_diff))
print(f"Batched GEMM time:    {elapsed_batched:.5f} sec")
print(f"Sequential GEMM time: {elapsed_sequential:.5f} sec")
print(f"Speedup: {elapsed_sequential / elapsed_batched:.2f}x")
```

This Batched GEMM consistently outpaces sequential execution, often by an order of magnitude or more. The library parallelizes the operations internally and takes advantage of GPU architecture, overlapping memory and compute for maximum utilization. This approach works efficiently for a wide range of batch sizes and matrix shapes, scaling from small experiments to production-scale workflows.

Using CuPy's 'dot' and 'matmul'

Introduction to CuPy's dot and matmul Functions

The CuPy provides familiar high-level functions for linear algebra: **cupy.dot** and **cupy.matmul**. These functions enable concise, expressive, and efficient mathematical operations on vectors and matrices. Under the hood, both functions leverage cuBLAS, so they are highly optimized for NVIDIA GPUs.

- The **cupy.dot** performs scalar (inner) products of vectors, matrix-vector multiplication, or matrix-matrix multiplication, depending on the shape of the inputs.
- And, the **cupy.matmul** is used for matrix multiplication, including support for broadcasting and batched operations on higher-dimensional arrays.

The use of the above functions means we do not need to write explicit loops or manage kernel launches, and we can focus on scientific or data analysis tasks while taking full advantage of GPU acceleration.

High-Level Vector and Matrix Operations

Vector Dot Product

We will compute the dot product of two large vectors:

```
import cupy as cp
import numpy as np
N = 500_000
a = cp.random.rand(N, dtype=cp.float32)
b = cp.random.rand(N, dtype=cp.float32)
# Dot product using CuPy
dot_result = cp.dot(a, b)
print("Dot product:", float(dot_result))
```

Matrix–Vector Multiplication

Suppose we have a matrix **A** and a vector **x**:

```
M, N = 1024, 1024
A = cp.random.rand(M, N, dtype=cp.float32)
x = cp.random.rand(N, dtype=cp.float32)
# Matrix-vector multiplication
y = cp.dot(A, x)
print("Matrix-vector result shape:", y.shape)
```

Matrix–Matrix Multiplication

We multiply two matrices using **dot** and **matmul** (both give the same result for 2D arrays):

```
K = 512
B = cp.random.rand(N, K, dtype=cp.float32)
# Matrix-matrix multiplication with dot
C1 = cp.dot(A, B)
print("Matrix-matrix result shape (dot):", C1.shape)
# Matrix-matrix multiplication with matmul
C2 = cp.matmul(A, B)
print("Matrix-matrix result shape (matmul):", C2.shape)
# Using the @ operator (same as matmul)
C3 = A @ B
print("Matrix-matrix result shape (@):", C3.shape)
```

Batched Matrix Multiplication with matmul

We will then compute matrix products across a batch dimension:

```
batch = 100
A_batch = cp.random.rand(batch, M, N, dtype=cp.float32)
B_batch = cp.random.rand(batch, N, K, dtype=cp.float32)
C_batch = cp.matmul(A_batch, B_batch)
print("Batched matrix-matrix shape:", C_batch.shape)  #
(batch, M, K)
```

The **cp.dot** handles vector dot products, matrix-vector multiplication, and 2D matrix-matrix multiplication. And, the **cp.matmul** (and **@**) generalize matrix multiplication for 2D and higher-dimensional (batched) arrays. Both functions are simple to use and call highly optimized GPU code internally, offering top-tier performance for all standard linear algebra workflows. By relying on these high-level routines, we can write clean, readable scientific code that harnesses the power of the GPU without manual optimization or kernel development.

Evaluating Numerical Accuracy

Throughout this chapter, we have accelerated linear algebra operations using the GPU, leveraging both custom kernels and highly optimized cuBLAS routines through CuPy. While the performance boost is often dramatic, it's also important to make sure that the results from GPU computations are consistent and reliable compared to traditional CPU-based workflows. The way floating-point arithmetic works on GPUs and CPUs can sometimes give you a slightly different result. This is because of things like different instruction ordering, precision, parallelism, and the use of fused operations.

It's really important to check the accuracy of your numbers, especially when they're used in other scientific or engineering calculations. In this topic, we're going to compare GPU and CPU outputs using standard error metrics.

Prepare Identical Inputs for CPU and GPU

We will work with a representative example—a matrix–matrix multiplication.

```
import numpy as np
import cupy as cp
M, N, K = 512, 512, 512
A_cpu = np.random.rand(M, N).astype(np.float32)
B_cpu = np.random.rand(N, K).astype(np.float32)
A_gpu = cp.array(A_cpu)
B_gpu = cp.array(B_cpu)
```

We then compute results on CPU and GPU:

```
# CPU result (NumPy)
C_cpu = np.dot(A_cpu, B_cpu)
# GPU result (CuPy, uses cuBLAS)
C_gpu = cp.dot(A_gpu, B_gpu)
C_gpu_cpu = cp.asnumpy(C_gpu)  # Bring result back to CPU for
comparison
```

Evaluate Error Metrics

There are several standard ways to measure the difference between two numerical arrays:

- **Maximum Absolute Error (L-infinity norm)** gives the largest absolute difference between any two corresponding elements.

- The **Root Mean Squared Error (L2 norm)** provides the square root of the mean of squared differences.
- And, the **Relative Error** is nothing but the error scaled by the norm (magnitude) of the reference.

Now, in the below, we will compute each of them:

```
abs_diff = np.abs(C_cpu - C_gpu_cpu)
max_error = np.max(abs_diff)
rmse = np.sqrt(np.mean((C_cpu - C_gpu_cpu) ** 2))
relative_error = rmse / np.linalg.norm(C_cpu)
print(f"Max absolute error: {max_error:e}")
print(f"Root mean squared error: {rmse:e}")
print(f"Relative error (L2 norm): {relative_error:e}")
```

For higher precision or critical workflows, consider using **`float64`** (double precision), but keep in mind that many consumer GPUs are optimized for **`float32`** and may be slower in double precision. This process is an essential step in scientific computing workflows, reinforcing the reliability of accelerated GPU solutions.

Summary

In this chapter, we primarily focused on harnessing the power of the GPU for core linear algebra tasks and built a robust understanding of both low-level and high-level approaches. We began with an introduction to cuBLAS, learning how its optimized routines can dramatically accelerate dense vector and matrix operations beyond what's achievable with custom kernels. We then saw how easily we could invoke cuBLAS for vector addition, matrix–vector multiplication, and large matrix–matrix products, always with a keen eye on performance comparisons.

We then advanced to batched GEMM operations, illustrating how performing many multiplications at once unlocks even greater GPU throughput compared to sequential execution. By leveraging CuPy's **`dot`** and **`matmul`** interfaces, we were able to perform expressive, high-level linear algebra operations on vectors, matrices, and batches—while benefiting from the underlying speed of cuBLAS. Finally, we reinforced scientific rigor by carefully evaluating the numerical accuracy of GPU computations against trusted CPU results, using L2 norms and relative errors.

Index

R

S

T

U

V

W

Z

Index

R

S

T

U

V

W

Z

Thank You

www.ingramcontent.com/pod-product-compliance
Lightning Source LLC
Chambersburg PA
CBHW080216170726
48282CB00030B/1141
* 9 7 8 9 3 4 9 1 7 4 7 9 5 *